ZERO
WASTE
IN THE LAST BEST PLACE

ZERO WASTE

IN THE LAST BEST PLACE

A PERSONAL ACCOUNT AND
HOW-TO GUIDE ON LANDFILL-FREE LIVING

Bradley Edward Layton, PhD, PE

ZERO WASTE IN THE LAST BEST PLACE
A PERSONAL ACCOUNT AND HOW-TO GUIDE
ON LANDFILL-FREE LIVING

iUniverse books may be ordered through booksellers or by contacting:

iUniverse
1663 Liberty Drive
Bloomington, IN 47403
www.iuniverse.com
1-800-Authors (1-800-288-4677)

ISBN: 978-1-5320-2268-5 (sc)
ISBN: 978-1-5320-2269-2 (hc)
ISBN: 978-1-5320-2267-8 (e)

Library of Congress Control Number: 2017910497

Print information available on the last page.

iUniverse rev. date: 10/26/2017

Contents

Acknowledgments

J eff Kuehn, thank you for being an inspiration for this book. You once told me that you were going to go a full year without throwing anything away. I don't know whether you achieved this, but not to be outdone, I decided to attempt to stretch that year into a lifetime (landfill-free since 2010 and counting) exploring the land of YIMBY.

This work would not have been complete without the help and inspiration of local recycling and sustainability practitioners like Jeremy Drake, Bob Giordano, Chase Jones, Steve Nelson, Martin NoRunner, Elizabeth Schenk, Edi Stan, Professor Vicky Watson, and my local editor, Ginny Merriam.

Thanks to the owners and operators of the funny little recycling center outside Philadelphia that would charge a fantastic rate to their customers who would drive to a facility only to be faced with the nebulous and unguided task of sorting through a vast array of materials on their own. What a fantastic racket! With any luck, this little book will educate the homeowner and business owner on best practices for avoiding paying for such "services."

I also owe Shanta a debt of gratitude for reminding me not to waste too much of my own time on waste. Rather than wasting time on circular discussions, I turned toward Staples CEO Mark Barkley and his model of the circular economy. Thanks, Mark and Shanta!

Thanks to my parents. Oscar the Grouch is happier now, and the elephant is being consumed. Thank you, Nathan Hansen. Landfills will be the elephants dotting our landscape unless we have the courage to face them with the urban mining strategies you propose.

I also thank the operator of the Anaconda-Deer Lodge County Landfill, Timothy Flynn, for sharing with me his feelings of helplessness related to the overwhelming volumes of matter that he endlessly piles up every day.

Thanks also to Dennis Richards for coming to me in search of a solution to the ocean-bound plastic rivers formed by discarded water bottles from relief efforts in Haiti.

I owe the citizens of Missoula for absorbing my externalities. My neighbors in particular have borne witness to and borne with me in the YIMBY lifestyle.

This work was also made possible in part with grants from the United States Department of Labor under the TAACCCT III SWAMMEI grant under the guidance and leadership of Vida Wilkinson, Barry Good, Perry Brown, and the National Science Foundation Advanced Technology Education grant DUE-1400670.

Preface

YIMBY
Yes! In My Back Yard

When I was a child, the garbage man transfixed me. The truck pulls up, brakes squeal, and two strapping young men hop from their monkey bars and fling the week's refuse into the jaws of the waiting kraken. The driver actuates the hydraulics, hydrogen sulfide and methane belch from the gaping maw, and then the rulers of rubbish grab hold again, hanging in space above the suburban pavement to repeat their Sisyphean task at the neighbor's house ad infinitum. What adventure!

Now that I have grown to appreciate the consequences of four-hundred-plus parts per million (ppm) carbon dioxide and methane in planet Earth's atmosphere, plastics in the ocean, and groundwater pollution, I have come to question the romantic, carefree landfilling practices of yesteryear. Rather than sit back and admit to a stalemate, I decided to lean into the problem a little and see if I couldn't be the change that I and many others anxiously anticipate.

The turning point for me to turn away from the lure of the landfill came in the form of a scolding finger waved my way by one of those strapping young lads sometime in Fall 2011. I, like the famous revelers of Arlo Guthrie's "Alice's Restaurant," thought "one big pile of garbage must be better than two little piles" as I casually tossed a couple pounds of tampons, candy bar wrappers, and a vacuum bag into the kraken of Columbine Road in Missoula. With a gentle scold, I was reminded that I was not a paying customer of our local private landfilling service. I retreated sheepishly to my garage cave and vowed to remove myself from the landfill stream.

Although I have not been 100 percent successful, on balance I've diverted more matter from the landfill than I've contributed to it, having intercepted clothing, vacuum cleaners, railroad ties, lawn furniture, dishes, countless plastic bags filled with grass clippings, and numerous other artifacts and organics on their way to a methanous mountain of matter slowly growing on the northern edge of Missoula, Montana.

Having lived in the Land of YIMBY—*"yes* in my backyard" is the antithesis of the notorious NIMBY, *"not* in my backyard"—I've learned many lessons that I've striven to share in this text.

Since moving to Missoula, home of *A River Runs through It*, downtown surfing, epic fly-fishing, and numerous other outdoor adventures, in 2010, I have been landfill-free in this self-proclaimed Last Best Place. With one exception where time and sanitation did not allow, I have not placed any materials or artifacts into a waste stream that was headed directly for a landfill. The YIMBY philosophy has brought many materials and artifacts to my house, for the purposes of soil building, construction, or heating. This book is, thus, a tale of adventures in the Land of YIMBY and has been written in a spirit intended to encourage others to join.

Before heading into the stories and minutiae of hard-core recycling, let me share with you the basics of zero-landfill practices in a one-page, quick-start guide to help you and your family continue on your own path toward a sustainable future.

Quick-Start, 12-Step Guide to Becoming Landfill-Free

1. Make a vow to avoid putting anything in a landfill stream—that is, any place where it will become trash headed toward what we traditionally call the dump. This vow might seem daunting at first but quickly becomes its own reward once you've experienced its practicality and sustainability.

2. Swear off garbage can liners. These masks hide our waste and perpetuate the burying and piling up of plastics, metals, ceramics, clothing, topsoil, glass, paper, organics, food, and complex chemicals in what are perhaps better dubbed as "landfulls."

3. Start and maintain a compost pile, or partner with a neighbor who has one. This is *the* solution to diverting all organic material from the landfill and creating invaluable nutrient-rich topsoil that our planet is losing at an alarming rate.

4. If you have a backyard, build, buy, or barter for a chicken coop and get two or three chickens. They will eat their way through most of your kitchen scraps. They'll also entertain and feed you!

5. Put like materials with like materials. The goal is to touch it twice—once while the container, tissue, or wrapper is being used and once as you send the chunk of spent matter on its way to be repurposed.

6. Get to know your neighbors. You're bound to find someone as passionate about sustainability as you are. Swap trade secrets, materials, and various recycling tasks with him or her to build a strong and trusted network.

7. Be conscious of what you buy. It will help you avoid materials that can be challenging to recycle. Your home or apartment is merely a waypoint for the matter you bring into it. What comes in must go out eventually. You will determine the path of that Popsicle stick, chewing gum wrapper, pizza box, or sofa cushion. Each of these artifacts came from nature and will ultimately return to nature, either mindfully or by default.

8. Ensure that all your old clothes and fabrics make it to your local Goodwill or thrift store. Share this task with a neighbor. You might even find a treasure or two along the way.

9. Take old shipping and packaging materials to your local Shipping Depot or other packaging and shipping store. You're likely to be rewarded with a discount on your next transaction.

10. Put your unwanted items up on Freecycle, Craigslist, or eBay. If you're too busy, give them to someone who will. There is a market for absolutely everything.

11. Donate your used electronics to a local charity that accepts them. The precious metals in these old gadgets will be put into service again, rather than becoming toxic landfill sludge or a hazardous gas to be inhaled by an innocent pair of lungs halfway around the planet.

12. Organize a triage station in your garage, mudroom, shed, or other transition zone to clean up your recycling piles and to make sorting easier. This will be the laboratory that saves you $200–$400 per year—a buck a day for your commitment to sustainability.

1

The World without Us[1]

In the beginning, if in fact there was a beginning, there were no humans. That much we can agree upon. Before the dawn of humankind, stuff like light, matter, and a lot of empty space existed. After the supernova that gave birth to our galaxy exploded and cooled and our solar system began its spiral dance, our molten proto-Earth cooled from the waste matter of that fateful explosion of the heavier elements. These heavier elements, especially carbon, nitrogen, oxygen, and phosphorous, now constitute and fuel our metabolisms and our technologies[20].

As the Earth cooled further and the oceans condensed, the land came alive with a multitude of organisms, some of them light loving—plankton, algae, plants, and so on. Next to emerge was an equally impressive array of organisms who made a living eating these light lovers—platypuses, ducks, antelope, and the like[29]. In turn, the metabolic mode of carnivorism emerged. This new set of meat-eating organisms gleaned energy on the go. Sharks, lions, and old *T. rex* preferred their meals warm, fresh, and spunky. And most recently, our own ancestors emerged on the global scene as peculiar organisms capable of either eating or rendering edible nearly every living species on the planet[102]. Our leftovers are consequently consumed by a multitude of microorganisms that methodically munch their way through the biosphere's leftovers, and Earth's gravity and weather consumes and sequesters whatever remains.

---

[1] Section title inspired by Copyright Collection (Library of Congress) (2007), *The World without Us*, a documentary by Alan Weisman, after Weisman's book of the same title (2007).

Regardless of how it all started, we're here now living in what remains of The Garden (Figure 1.1) that may be mythically or historically considered as the last point at which humans lived without technology, or perhaps at the dawn of what some Big Historians are calling the Anthropocene[51, 21, 22]. This Garden Era, either mythical or literal, was also certainly a time when we lived much closer to thermodynamic equilibrium with our natural surroundings.[104]

FIGURE 1.1. Picture of The Garden of Eden with a vague reference to the food chain. Note the lack of waste receptacles (Jan Brueghel the Elder and Pieter Paul Rubens)[15].

With the invention of the first technologies such as the hand ax, we began partitioning the matter contained in nature into "goods" and "waste" in earnest.

Goods and *waste* are not terms to be taken lightly. They are relative terms, of course. That sandwich wrapper, which is on its way to becoming *waste*, was quite *good* at keeping mayonnaise off your silk scarf. The ceramic butter dish that you just dropped on the tile floor had served you well for decades, did it not? Nevertheless, the sandwich wrapper and the broken dish are now part of your waste stream. But what to do with them? For the majority of modern Americans, the answer is to simply throw them "away."

But away to where? As it turns out, "away" is getting closer all the time. We'll look into the fast-approaching erosion of the boundaries separating humankind and our waste in detail shortly through the eyes of sustainability guru[17]. For now, though, start to think of "away" as literally being out of sight, either down or up—*buried* or *burned*. Everything else is in between and still here, being *built* with.

Some of our more recent ancestors who left The Garden proceeded to invent a vast array of ways to harness the physical process known as combustion—or, in common parlance, fire—to make life safer, more comfortable, and all-around much better for themselves[11,39]. These combustion technologies, such as woodstoves, steam engines, internal combustion engines, coal-fired power plants, and so on, not only made life safer and more secure for a substantial number of individuals of our own species but also made many otherwise hazardous foods palatable and safe to eat through the practice of cooking[100].

Eventually, money was invented, and for many humans who possessed the wherewithal to harness fire and technology, this trait generated tremendous monetary and material wealth for those who wrought them either to develop agricultural technologies or weapons technologies[32,70]. Through fits and starts, the Industrial Revolution eventually began, and the race was on to churn out bigger, more powerful, smarter, and deadlier technologies (Figure 1.2).

FIGURE 1.2. An example of early industrial technologies (Ruston Proctor Steam Engine Erecting Shop, c. 1910).[2]

Many of these technologies, such as forges, looms, and kilns, were capable of consuming materials and converting them into artifacts. We had become so good at using the thermal energy released by fire to create useful materials and artifacts that we continued to do so, eventually finding even more exotic materials and modes of sculpting fire to craft the technologies that we know, love, and in some cases literally cannot live without (Figure 1.3).

Despite their life-saving, life-giving, and life-enhancing power, all the technologies depicted below and indeed *all* technologies will ultimately meet their fate of being worn out and, thus, destined to be piled up or disassembled and distilled to their constituent elements.

Recycling happens, either intentionally and mindfully in the present or "naturally" and valuelessly and, in some cases, harmfully in the future. What remains to be seen is whether nature will be able to process our waste in a sustainable manner or whether we will be further compelled to stay ahead of ourselves on the overflowing conveyor belt of mounting waste streams we produce.

---

[2] http://www.oldengine.org/members/ruston/History1.htm

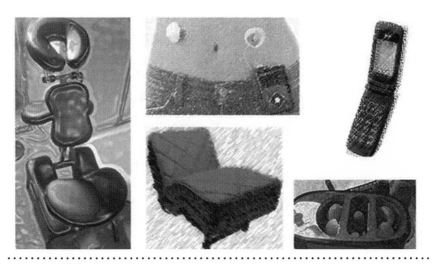

FIGURE 1.3. Massage chairs, insulin pumps, cell phones, adjustable beds, and hot dog toasters represent technologies that have emerged very recently, are made of a large number of materials and components, and will ultimately have the fate of being worn out and thus destined for the landfill or a recycling stream.

Our progression of cutting meat from bone, separating wheat from chaff, and now engineering the fabric of life itself to serve our metabolic needs has run in parallel with our technological ability to extract ores from rock, to forge knives and fashion boards and bowls from trees, and to liquefy oxygen from air itself to keep sick lungs from failing.

As nanotechnologists, we have now begun sifting through DNA fragments, purifying drugs, and sorting other small molecules at the nanoscale level in the medical and related fields. This sorting, separating, and purifying requires energy, and the primary challenge for coming generations will be how to continue sorting safely, efficiently, and harmoniously without taxing the biosphere to the point of collapse.

Throughout history, we have always faced the persistent problem of ridding ourselves of and processing our own personal *biological waste*. Ineffective disposal and treatment of toxins or infectious agents leaving our bodies has resulted in and continues to lead to disease—cholera, food poisoning, MRSA, and on and on.

We now battle and frequently defeat microscopic organisms that are fighting fiercely for their own survival by either eating or taking up residence in whatever biomass they can invade. Many leaps forward in science have been the result of exploiting microorganisms such as *Thermus aquaticus, Saccharomyces cerevisiae,* and *Penicillium chrysogenum.* One key to sustainable waste practices is the understanding and exploitation of the metabolic pathways of these microorganisms so that they can do the nanoscale sorting for us. At the end of the day, though, biology is simply a complex combination of carbon, hydrogen, oxygen, nitrogen, and a few other inert key elements[13,18,26,41,48,50,54,56,59,60,64,96,99,108,110,121,133,137].

Ineffective disposal, treatment, and repurposing of *technological waste* can lead to ecological collapse when organisms large and small become overly burdened with molecules, elements, and compounds they are not equipped to metabolize. Here in Montana, the tailings from the Berkeley Pit in Butte resulted in fish kills and poisoned water in the Clark Fork River[86]. Much has been written on the irresponsible and negligent handling of technological waste and how it has affected Montana's waterways. For further reading on this topic see the additional resources section[16,34,57,94,103,109,126].

Coal ash, comprised of the incombustible matter in coal, continues to be a problem for large energy companies[27]. Another waste stream of the fossil fuel era results in plastics in rivers and oceans that kills marine life[35,79,120,138]. It appears as if we may be creating waste streams faster than nature can adapt to create a solution to sustainably metabolize them. For example, there are no known enzymes that break the polyethylene bonds found in #2 and #4 plastics. Given enough time, nature will most likely invent this capability. She has already invented genetic codes to manufacture enzymes that break down complex carbonaceous polymers such as collagen and cellulose.

Philosophical and futuristic arguments aside, waste *is* inevitable, and, like most problems, we can deal with it now in a transparent manner or deal with it later in strife. The thesis of *Zero Waste in the Last Best Place* is that choosing the former is not only doable, it's rewarding and entertaining: We must deal with the waste stream now and turn packaging, broken artifacts, kitchen scraps, and yard waste into other valuable goods, such as soil, new artifacts, dwellings, or energy.

Recycling, just like any hobby or obsession, requires time, effort, and energy. Time is a gift you are given at birth. The effort comes from your will to create a world of abundance rather than scarcity. The energy to recycle is your own as you take the extra steps to find the proper bin, supplemented by grinders, shredders, and manufacturing equipment powered by renewable or nonrenewable sources.

Fundamentally, all the *primary energy* we consume comes from one of four sources—the sun's radiation, radioactive decay, the gravitational sloshing of the seas, or the residual heat of tectonic settling. Of these, the only truly renewable energies have their origins in the photons that have blessed our planet within the past few decades and that are at wavelengths that drive photosynthesis[113]. The non-renewables, such as carbon-rich coal, oil, and natural gas also resulted from photosynthesis, but during eras well before our species was even a glimmer in Gaia's eye.

Game Changers: Diamond, Friedman, Hansen, Running et al.

Civilizations have been rising and falling for millennia, with technological progress leapfrogging us toward longer, more secure, and more comfortable lives. But a couple of decades ago, one of the members of our species known as James Hansen, who had been hired by the National Aeronautics and Space Administration to look at global weather patterns, was looking at some photographs that had been taken from far above our planet's surface. After comparing recent images to those that had been taken several years prior, James Hansen began wondering, "Hey, what happened to all the ice?" (Figure 1.4).

Others among us have traveled the globe documenting the effects that our nascent technologies are having on the natural world[63,125,132]. For a visual narrative on the effects that technology has had on the natural landscape, consider watching *Koyaanisqatsi,* the first film in filmmaker Godfrey Reggio's trilogy conveying his apocalyptic vision of the collision of two worlds, urban life/technology and the natural environment[52].

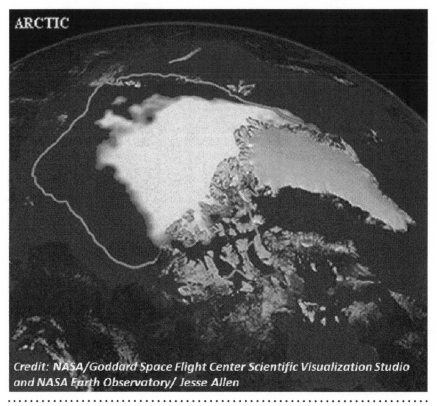

FIGURE 1.4. Picture of reduced ice mass[3]. The nearly forty billion tons of waste CO_2 that we pump into the atmosphere each year now has a concentration of more than four hundred parts per million. This relatively high level has not been present in the last million years, maybe not in the last twenty-five million years.

Hansen put his day job in jeopardy with his observations, was censored, and was finally arrested for publically protesting national energy policy or lack thereof [45]. Others among us, such as Steve Running, began to take notice[62,73,111]. Running and others made an effort to tell the rest of our species of the perils that may await if we continue to rely upon *fire* to make our lives more comfortable, but by that time, it was too late for many. Other members of our fantastically successful species, such as Thomas Friedman and Jared Diamond have also taken big-picture views and proclaimed both dire warnings and optimistic prescriptions of the trajectory our species will take on this planet[32,33,47]. Even climate-change skeptics such as Ronald

---

[3] http://www.nasa.gov/topics/earth/features/arctic-antarctic-ice.html.

Bailey have recently acknowledged the need to begin limiting greenhouse gas emissions[5]. And while many members of our species look for reasons other than combustion technologies[4] to explain the rapid warming of the atmosphere, we can simply look to simple engineering physics equations for a glimpse into the future[67,68,69,70,71,72].

As its title implies, *Zero Waste in the Last Best Place* is not about climate change, global warming, or geoscience. There are other books about those topics. The practice of landfilling exacerbates climate change[87]. This book questions the appropriateness of the use of technologies such as the one pictured in Figure 1.5 as a means of *progress* in our postindustrial age.

FIGURE 1.5. Typical garbage truck.[5] Is this really the way forward? We can and must do better, especially in the Last Best Place.

And while landfills such as the one pictured in Figure 1.6 do contribute their methane to the atmosphere, this book is not about pointing out

---

[4] This is left as an exercise for the reader: Find peer-reviewed articles that refute anthropogenic climate change by going to Web of Science (http://www. webofknowledge.com).

[5] http://nypost.com/2014/02/23/garbage-truck-strikes-kills-pedestrian/.

problems. There are also plenty of books that do that. Rather, *Zero Waste in the Last Best Place* is about the rate at which humans produce waste, where it goes, where it shouldn't go, what can be done to rechannel it, and how to turn trash into treasure. This concept, as well as solutions for collectively moving forward to a cleaner, greener future has recently been discussed by Lovins and others[78].

FIGURE 1.6. Typical landfill. Even in the Last Best Place, Montana, birds flock over our Mount Methane, feasting on bits of rotting food waste, ingesting plastic, and sickening our garden valley. Photo credit: Jeremy Drake.

FIGURE 1.7. Aerial view of Missoula's landfill, a.k.a. Mount Methane. Waste Management is currently advertising that it has created thousands of acres of wildlife habitat. Will this be the decades-timescale fate of our landfill as well?

The images in Figures 1.3 through 1.7 depict the mixing of food (the result of very recent sunshine, rain, and a lot of hard work) with ancient hydrocarbons (the result of very ancient sunshine, rain, and a heck of a lot of geological activity) that predate The Garden. Piling new biomass with this ancient biomass makes as much sustainable sense as Homer Simpson standing in front of his refrigerator to stay cool[6] or, in the author's opinion, burning ancient biomass in the form of gasoline to make one's grass blades all the same height.

I recently received a signed copy of a book written by Ted Carns through a four-degrees-of-separation connection, and an instant bond was formed. As I read through *Off On Our Own* I was immediately excited by the reality that there was another person out there like me who was making an all-out attempt at sustainable waste utilization[17]. My initial enthusiasm turned to awe as I learned of Ted's accomplishments. On his little Stone Camp in central Pennsylvania, he has not only managed to integrate the cast-offs of others—wood, chainsaws, hand tools, soil, and so on—into his domicile; he has also managed to be extremely productive. Ted makes his own maple

---

[6] https://www.youtube.com/watch?v=ioyU_sZufC8.

syrup, ferments his own wine, and grows a broad range of vegetables. His efforts at sustainability are truly epic.

A big point that Ted Carns makes in *Off On Our Own* is that his path is *not the only path* but merely the one that became necessary for him once he made the commitment to move toward a lifestyle that was less dependent on conventional mercantile spheres. Another big message in Carns's book was his mantra that we must simultaneously be the masters of our environment as well as its humble stewards. He concluded with the observation that needlessly and carelessly throwing things "away" is the equivalent of material bigotry.

If you're near a computer now or reading this online, take a look at the reviews of *Off On Our Own*. What you will find is that they are bimodal; many people found the book to be enlightening and awakening. Many others said that it was a waste of time and did not provide enough "how-to" but was more of a "philosophy lesson." The upshot is that there is no single answer or silver bullet on how to live more sustainably. Each of us must find our path and our place within the intricate environmental and economic web that our global civilization is rapidly weaving, unraveling, and restringing.

If we rewind the clock of history before the Age of Stuff [77], we would immediately notice that the artifacts of our recent ancestors had very recently been part of nature—bones, skin, rocks, and sticks. Once we had finished with them, they would return to the earth and reenter the biosphere relatively quickly and seamlessly. There are still regions of the planet that have not seen actual human contact, but I'm still unpleasantly surprised every time I see a plastic wrapper or a cigarette butt way off the beaten path on a mountain trail near the Last Best Place.

In The World Without Us, nothing goes to waste. In the absence of technology, all molecules are organic and will thus find their ways back into the biosphere. Perhaps that plastic-eating bacterium postulated above will emerge naturally, or maybe we will engineer one. But for now the necessity of dealing with technological waste is a challenge that will continue to beg for a solution.

On average, humans produce 1.5 pounds of solid waste per person per day[83]. For North Americans, this is closer to 4 to 5 pounds per day. Lovins and Wernick and Ausubel estimate that industry moves, extracts, processes, and uses twenty times each person's body weight per person per day[78,149].

The number *twenty* happens to be a convenient mnemonic, as it is also the approximate number of technological slaves that the average *Homo sapiens sapiens* has working for him- or herself around the clock 24/7, 365 days a year[67]. Technically speaking, someone with a 2,500-calorie diet eats ten megajoules of energy per day[7]. The average human living today also consumes or converts two hundred megajoules of primary energy into heat per day.

Before we fully immerse ourselves in a material waste discussion, let's first take a moment to discuss energetic waste. On an annual basis, humans convert five hundred exajoules[8] of mostly carbonaceous chemical energy into forms that serve our needs—lifting things, heating and lighting our homes, making stuff, moving around, and on and on. *All* these 500 exajoules of chemical energy become thermal. Since energy cannot be created or destroyed, it must go somewhere. As it turns out, that somewhere is everywhere. Thermal energy is very leaky. Heat from a hot object will always find a way to radiate, convect, or conduct its way to colder objects, and most of this thermal energy finds its way to our atmosphere as shown in the equation on page 139.

With this in mind, let's begin to develop technologies that make use of waste heat from washing machines, dishwashers, and other appliances. Let's send it under our roads to melt ice or keep it under our homes to keep us warm in winter so we can turn down the fracking tap. Use of some waste heat from combustion-based power plants is already being used in district heating. As we move away from large coal-fired power plants, we're likely to see more of this creative use of waste heat.

It's well known that the sun pumps energy at us approximately ten thousand times faster than we use it. So in a sense, 9,999 out of 10,000 photons from the sun are "wasted" in the form of wind and waves, which themselves result from heat left over from thermal gradients caused by the sun shining on Earth at different times and intensities. So let's phase out and abandon the coal mines as the United Kingdom has just done, pull up stakes

---

[7] As 1 calorie is 4,184 joules, 2,500 calories is about ten million joules.

[8] This is the equivalent of detonating twenty thousand bombs the size of the one dropped on Hiroshima every single day of every single year. Through a more energy-conscious approach, we can reign in this massacre of the atmosphere.

at the oil fields, quit fracking around, decarbonize our energy systems, and move bravely into a clean energy future.

One big step toward this future will require us to be more mindful of the boundary between the technosphere and the biosphere (Figure 1.8). In a sense, this should be relatively straightforward as we ourselves live within this boundary. Where is the boundary? It's at the edge of your back patio, beneath the tires of your mountain bike, on the soles of your boots, stuck to the bristles of your hairbrush, and inside your vacuum bags.

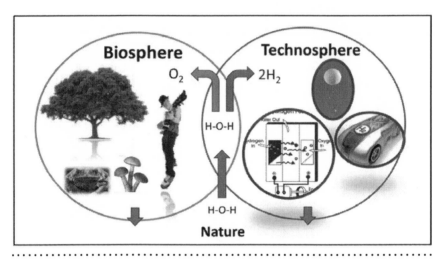

FIGURE 1.8. Biosphere vs. technosphere vs. nature (B, T, N). In this figure, the flow of one water molecule is depicted as flowing among the biosphere, the technosphere, and nature. We humans are, of course, a portion of the biosphere, but our modern lives depend on the developments, maintenance, and innovations of the technosphere.

Exercises

1. Make an estimate of the amount of solid waste that you create each day. Take a photo of the things you discard. What is the volume? What is the mass?

2. Make an estimate of the amount of energy you consume metabolically each day. Express this number in joules. For example, a one-hundred-calorie beverage contains 418,400 joules.

3. Research James Hansen and Steve Running. What are their degrees? What do they measure? Are they driven by financial gain in a manner similar to that of a CEO of a major corporation?
4. Does landfill reduction matter? Haven't landfills been put to good use by creating landmass in Boston and New York?
5. Can't landfills be used to generate methane and, thus, electricity? How do carbon emissions play into a waste-to-energy model?
6. Why focus on eliminating the use of landfills when we should really be focusing on reducing our reliance on fossil fuels? What are your own sustainability priorities and how do they interact?

2

Artifacts vs. Materials

After more than seven years of landfill-free living and renewable energy technology development, the modus operandi of my students, colleagues, and I has become apparent. We strive to derive as much utility from waste or any material artifact as possible while minimizing the drain on our own energetic and temporal resources. More simply, we squeeze as much utility out of a given object or material as possible before sending it downstream. A key piece in this sustainability puzzle is the minimization of environmental impacts.

It is thus a triple-bottom-line approach: (1) Maximize the utility of materials and artifacts. (2) Minimize deleterious effects on one's own being. (3) Minimize environmental damage.

If our zero-waste strategy serendipitously augments or preserves the environment, financially or spiritually rewards us, and stuff isn't wasted, then it's a triple bottom-line win-win-win!

A good place to start this practice is with the humble container—glass, metal, paper, or plastic will do. As a container at the grocery store, the glass bottle facilitates the logistics of moving the contents of the bottle to the consumer. It gives the producer control over contamination, shelf life, and portion size. It gives the retailer predictability in planning for inventory, shelf allotment, and sales quantity. It gives the consumer the convenience of not having to do his or her own packaging, as well as a temporary vessel in which the product can be stored in the refrigerator or pantry prior to or during consumption. With its contents consumed, the container is now either an asset or a liability. If a liability, the consumer will typically pay a curbside service to haul it to the landfill or recycling center. At seven pounds per person per day and a typical four-person household, we can get rid of an average of thirty pounds of matter for a buck (three cents a pound). If the empty jar is an asset, it continues to store and organize other materials or artifacts.

If the container has no perceived value as an artifact, it still has value as a material. Crushed, baled, and shipped metal cans become new metallic artifacts. Glass bottles are reborn into building materials. Paper containers transform into energy, compost, or even water and carbon. Whether the artifact is repurposed as is, or returned to its material stream, time and energy are required. It is our job as zero wasters, a.k.a. zee dubbers (pronounced "zee dubbers") to determine how to minimize the time and energy required to move the artifact to its next state so that the personal bottom line stays light.

Triage: Many Paths Lead from the Bottom to the Top

If you've ever been to the hospital or know someone who works in the health industry, you've probably heard the word *triage*. This word has its roots in the French *trier* for "pick out" and in other earlier languages, where it reflected the ideas of tearing apart. I typically think of it as standing at the fork of a single incoming stream that splits into two streams and then four and so on (as depicted in Figure 2.1). A more appropriate name might be bifurcation, but if Pittsburgh can get away with calling the Ohio River the Allegheny River, and the Monongahela River "Three Rivers," we should be fine using the word *triage* as a general term for making a decision about how to take a constant stream of waste with varying sizes, masses, and material composition and separating it into an arbitrarily large number of smaller streams of valuable artifacts and materials.

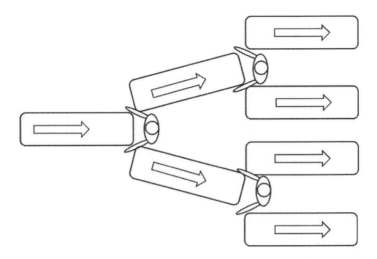

FIGURE 2.1. Basic idea behind triaging. Conveyor belts or simple tables bring materials and artifacts toward a human or mechanical sorter, who then moves materials and artifacts into various subcategories. A more sophisticated sorting system might have a single user sorting into multiple streams rather than two. See chapter 10 for a list of categories available worldwide.

What distinguishes an artifact from a material? Think of it this way—all squares are rectangles, but not all rectangles are squares. By the same token, all artifacts are made of materials, but not all materials become artifacts. For example, glass, the material, only becomes a glass artifact when blown into the shape of a bottle, molded into a drinking glass, poured to become a window pane, or drawn into an optic fiber and so on. Aluminum is only an artifact if it takes the shape of a beverage can, a bicycle frame, an airplane fuselage, or some other object. Typically, the more time and effort spent shaping a material, the greater its value; wooden boat hulls are more valuable than wood paneling; plastic eyeglass lenses are more valuable than plastic clothes hangers, and so on and so forth.

Big Picture: Recycling Writ Large

The recycling symbol has been around since 1969, and while its original message was "reduce, reuse, recycle," I like to think of it as a symbol that represents the conservation of matter and energy (Figure 2.2). Nothing escapes this perpetual churn.

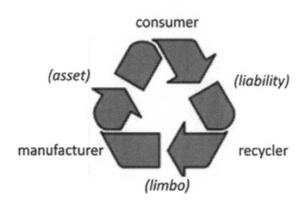

....

FIGURE 2.2. The original recycling symbol stands for reduce, reuse, recycle. Another way to look at it is with the consumer sitting at the top of the triangle, extracting value from the material or artifact. Once used, we shuffle materials along the bottom leg of the triangle via various recycling streams, where manufacturers add value through thermal, mechanical, and chemical processes to create consumable artifacts. The lower right corner represents the activity typically known as recycling. Imagine every possible material and artifact being shuttled along the bottom of the triangle either in small, purified fragments or as whole artifacts, such as clothing, furniture, vehicles, and the like. The bottom left corner represents the injection of energy and ingenuity to create another product for the consumer, taking a liability and turning it into an asset *ad infinitum*.

The next level of complexity of the model, shown in Figure 2.3, comes into play when money is involved, thus accelerating the rate at which matter moves through markets. If we are to achieve a zero-waste civilization, greater complexity and knowledge of physical chemistry must emerge to turn even the smallest fragments of waste into tiny treasures for trade. Indeed, proper monetization is the most likely way that zero-waste recycling will become truly sustainable.

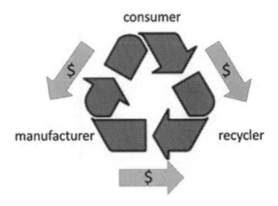

consumer

manufacturer

recycler

FIGURE 2.3. For recycling to be economically sustainable under our current market conditions, the consumer and the manufacturer must pay the recycler for his or her time, transportation, triage, and storage, while the manufacturer pays the recycler for his or her artifacts and materials. The manufacturer recovers his or her costs when the consumer makes a purchase. See chapter 3, Artifacts for a discussion on debunking comments from the naysayers who are yet to see the value and validity of this model.

Just as artifacts are made of materials, molecules are made of atoms. At both the macroscale and the atomic scale, energy must typically be injected into matter for building and assembly to occur. Building a car from glass, metal, rubber, and plastic requires an expenditure of energy. So does the assembly of a glucose molecule from carbon, oxygen, and hydrogen. Nanomachines called enzymes are manufacturing molecules in your body right now, and fleets of cells are building and maintaining tissues from larger molecules. In fact, as much as 50 percent of your 2,500-calorie-per-day metabolic diet may be devoted to molecular synthesis, with the remainder devoted to muscular motor function and molecular trafficking and pumping. It is the promise of the bioindustrial complex to put these highly specialized molecular machines to work in the emerging circular economy.

The same is true for artificial synthesis. Energy must be added to smaller components such as atoms or entire assemblies to put them together. For artifacts such as aluminum cans, there is an embodied energy in creating the requisite aluminum alloy. Invariably, the production of materials requires that they become hot for both the requisite diffusion and active transport of impurities out of a substance or for the introduction of the required alloying elements. In other words, to move junk atoms out of a pure substance, they need energy to move. We perform this type of energy injection daily. Doing the dishes or laundry injects chemical, mechanical, and thermal energy to move soils from surfaces and fabrics. Injecting thermal, mechanical, and chemical energy into a baking cake enables it to assemble in the pan and oven. We promptly resoil our dishes and clothes while the energy in the cake becomes chemical, electrical, mechanical, and thermal energy inside our bodies ad infinitum.

Examples of materials include all currently known elements and essentially any combination thereof, either natural or synthetic. Gold, aluminum, oxygen, zinc, and the like, are examples of *elemental* materials. Wood, stone, water, air, dirt, and so on, are *natural* materials. Glass, high-density polyethylene, cardboard, latex, and such are examples of *synthetic* materials.

Artifacts, on the other hand, are assemblies of materials—lamps, chairs, hammers, cars, soda cans, tires, shirts, shoes, trash cans, napkins, mirrors, lamps, drywall sheets, two-by-fours, lemon squeezers, eyeglasses, window blinds, airplanes, corkscrews, the Space Shuttle, the Eiffel Tower, and the Great Wall of China. It is therefore the recycler's dilemma as to whether an artifact that no longer has any value to the owner is better off banked, bartered, or bought. We will visit this fundamental economic topic in chapter 5. The fundamental question for you, the zee dubber, is whether the artifact is more valuable in its present form or whether it will be of greater value once distilled into its chemical and elemental components.

As noted earlier, as long as there is either conscious (human-driven) or unconscious (naturally-driven) competition for resources[20], the universe will remain in motion. All the subsystems of the universe will remain in motion, whether this means the electrons in orbit around their nuclei or the planets around their stars. This does not leave much room for humans to slow down or relax as we compete for perceived limited resources, whether they be food, money, love, sex, real estate, or other material wealth. We ourselves cannot simply hibernate. There is no perpetual state of homeostasis. We therefore continuously process matter and energy to avoid entropic collapse[114]. We will, therefore, always produce waste. As conscious, sentient beings, we face a decision every time we exhaust an artifact—deal with it now, keeping our material or artifact in the biosphere or technosphere and thus the econosphere, or pile it up in a landfill (Chapter 7) and allow it to decompose into a toxic methane sludge bomb.

Every technology will fail or eventually become obsolete[84]. Mechanical failure is typically caused by a material being stressed or heated to the point where molecular bonds fail and come apart, leading to the loss of a thermal or pressure gradient. Our own deaths are typically the result of similar failure mechanisms—heart attack, aneurism, and so on. Our bodies do have a nanomechanical means of non-catastrophic failure known as apoptosis, but my point is that, once biological or technological death occurs, the matter that constituted the biological or technological system will then be either actively or passively recycled. The practice of landfilling falls somewhere between active and passive. Think of it as active procrastination that must be avoided in order to achieve a higher level of environmental and economic sustainability.

Exercises

1. Take a picture of the stuff in your garage. What fraction has value as artifacts? What fraction has value as materials?
2. How might you configure your garage to streamline the triaging of items that you need to get rid of?
3. What is the total dollar value of all the artifacts in your garage? To you? To someone else?
4. Do you have a storage unit? Hold an auction, take the cash, and pay off your debts.
5. What were the three aspects of the triple bottom line mentioned in this chapter?
6. Who can you reach out to who would take your material and artifact waste off your hands without a fee? Who might you pay to take them away?

3

Artifacts

What Are Artifacts?

As mentioned in the previous chapter, an artifact is a specific configuration of a material—a molded plastic mug, a folded and glued paper carton, or any assembly of materials that serves as a technology, such as a coffee thermos made from metal and plastic or a baseball made from rubber, twine, and leather.

Perhaps the first prominent human artifact was the hand ax. This single technology was a one-piece artifact constructed from what otherwise would be considered as waste rock. So why bother making the hand ax in the first place? What's wrong with a regular old rock one might find on the ground? What leads us to dream up, design, and manufacture the dizzying array of artifacts that comprise our built environment?

Time and effort spent in making the hand ax must have had an enormous energy returned on energy invested (EROEI) ratio. Even if we assume that the hand ax would take a full work week to construct, these forty hours, representing fifty megajoules of human energy, would pay back roughly one thousand-fold in protein and fat, not to mention resources such as bone, hide, and organs for making additional artifacts once the hand ax had been successfully used to kill a large animal.

Many hand axes still lay littered among abandoned watering holes in Africa (Figure 3.1).[9] There are also examples of discarded items from more recent human societies in regions of North America. These minilandfills,

---

[9] http://www.indiana.edu/~origins/teach/P314/lectures/Oct28.html.

known as middens (Figure 3.2) are protected by Canadian law, presumably for their value in allowing us to peer into the dietary and technological habits of our ancestors[3,25,61,66,74,81,88,89,90,98,107,116,117,130,145].

FIGURE 3.1. Hand axes[10] were likely used for a variety of tasks, including digging, but most likely the most prevalent use was being launched by hand on a ballistic trajectory toward a large, four-legged, unsuspecting ungulate as it drank from a watering hole in Africa. The time and effort put into constructing such an artifact would have a huge EROEI.

---

[10] http://phys.org/news/2009-09-giant-stone-age-axes-african-lake.html.

FIGURE 3.2. Photo of the author's compost pile to simulate middens found in the San Juan Islands. Notice some shells and bones. Will our present-day landfills one day serve as archeological heritage sites? Can you imagine paying an admission fee to tour the bowels of the landfills we are building as you read this?

More than likely there were a few individual members of our early tribal ancestors who were better at crafting the valuable hand ax than others. It could have been that these individuals were among the more powerful and influential within the tribe. Or perhaps these gifted individuals were exploited and undervalued in the same way that some of our talented contemporary artisans and craftspeople are. Either way, the toolmakers were specialists and must have found their niche within the prefiduciary economy of our ancestors.

Eventually money was invented, and economies became more complex, as did tools[9,68,91,101]. We of course now sell tools as commodities with the assumption that wealth will flow back to the toolmaker for his or her contribution to the ever-accelerating pace of complexity and interdependence among humans[127,128]. Now, of course, we also have tools to make tools, rather than carving, molding, or casting them by hand and one by one. The same mass production and EROEI calculus applies.

This point was even brought to bear in the recent bestseller *Boys in the Boat*, which reminds us that Henry Rantz's father was forced out of the car-building business by Henry Ford[12]. With the recent advances in 3-D printing technology, however, our machines that make artifacts are allowing us to custom-make one-off parts and even recreate parts for which the original dies are either long since gone or unavailable.

One unfortunate side effect of mass production and competition among toolmakers and other artifact makers is that planned obsolescence trumps durability. All engineering curricula contain some type of design course, where young engineering students learn the equations for friction, wear, fracture, fatigue, oxidation, and the like. The mastery of these rules serves one of two ends—(1) design the artifact in such a way that the integrity of its physical state will outlive its owner (titanium bicycle frames, solid maple cutting boards, cast iron kettles) or (2) design the artifact in such a way that it breaks just after the warranty expires (fifty-dollar bicycle-shaped objects from Wal-Mart, plastic-handled dish scrubbers, Teflon-coated pans).

Some craftspeople and companies still strive on a motto of making products built to last indefinitely or have an economic policy in place that enables them to replace warn artifacts with new ones at no additional cost to the consumer after the original purchase. Craftsman has had this policy for years, as has Rigid Tool Company.

Toys

No discussion on artifacts would be complete without a look at toys, which range from expensive, complex robotic kits to the ubiquitous, versatile, and humble cardboard box. Any simple artifact that offers manual dexterity lessons for building rich dense neural circuits at a young age is likely to serve children later in life when they tackle temporal-spatial problems such as aircraft maintenance or cello playing. A task as simple as untangling a knotted piece of string gives a child an opportunity to develop fine motor skills and a close connection with the material world.

Coincidently, a close friend and mentor of mine recently shared an idea to create toys that charge, rather than drain batteries. Such technology already exists in some soccer balls, but what about building charging systems into pogo sticks, hockey pucks, and even board games? This would continue an existing trend toward greater efficiency and utility of energy that would otherwise go to waste.

When it comes to triaging, toys may be among some of the most difficult artifacts to part with, at least psychologically. Think about all the sentimental items you still own from your childhood, some handed down from previous generations. Even the worn Raggedy Ann doll has a special shelf in the house or a special box in a closet. What to do with these treasures? Since some toys never actually wear out completely, the issue of triaging toys is a persistent one, tied up with both financial and emotional economics. Dolls may lose their stuffing or get a tear here or there. The toy soldier's paint wears off or an arm comes unglued, but short of flood or fire, toys are immortal.

Given the nature of most toys, building something creative from their remnants seems to be preferable to burying or burning them. If you ever watched *Treehouse Masters*, you may have seen the episode where a woman had a tree house insulated with old blue jeans. Do the same with your old fabric toys. Use them as a sort of time capsule to insulate your home after consulting with a fire protection engineer or donate them to a Goodwill or thrift shop, many of which have zero-landfill policies.

I'm in the process of converting 8 Columbine Road in Missoula into a net-positive home that will ultimately become a resource center for those seeking sustainability ideas or a haven for someone looking to move away from fossil fuels. Part of this process compelled me to undertake the somber task of moving many of my children's toys and games from their childhood rooms. With a feeling of ennui, I simply left much of these artifacts on the front walk, under the eave, but out of the elements (Figure 3.3). Sure enough, the young neighbor boys dropped by and began drooling over these treasures. I invited them to dig in. The latest report is that they are honing their chess skills with the Lego chessboard that my son Blake and I used to enjoy.

Again, there really is no shortage of options when it comes to recycling toys. Donate them to a local day care. Send them to a children's shelter. Let the dog chew 'em up! Glue them to an old car! When I lived in Ann Arbor during my graduate school years, I would frequently spot cars that were literally covered in old toys. There was a lizard and dinosaur car and a rubber ducky car with little Mickey Mouse figurines glued here and there. What fun it is to keep it weird!

. . . .
FIGURE 3.3. As I write this, my family is in transition. Several old toys that are on their way to donation await their fate. I also grabbed a few fluorescent lightbulbs to take to the University of Montana, which has a centralized processing center for heavy metal waste.

Random, Unidentifiable Parts

Some parts defy categorization (Figure 3.4). For these, your choices are similar to those related to toys and clothes. You can decide that the artifact deserves another look as an artifact and then pack it away in a labeled drawer or decide that it's worth its weight in garbage and chuck it into the most appropriate material stream. Typically, this will be plastic, paper, or some composite thereof. In many cases, the part is small enough for a time capsule. The stone wall I'm building in my backyard has a ways to go, so the wall itself has become a perfect receptacle for sequestering domestic detritus. The wall might not end up being King Tut's Tomb, but as Richard Feynman announced over a half century ago, "there's plenty of room at the bottom." My burying of these little nontoxic trinkets is just one temporary fate of discarded technology within our ever-expanding technosphere.

FIGURE 3.4. Random parts. This is ground zero in my garage triage area after a few weeks of accumulation. Visible are computer cases, wine corks, plastic lids, small wrappers, twist ties, and even a leaf. Most of these items will head to the technosphere in their respective material streams.

As part of my autumn 2015 Recycling Technology course, which I developed with assistance from the Department of Labor, I allowed each of my students to select his or her favorite material or artifact to focus on recycling or repurposing. One student selected the ubiquitous TetraPak (Figure 3.5). Ideas we developed for pumping new life into these sturdy and well-designed artifacts are (1) using them as bioreactors for sequestering carbon dioxide or producing methane; (2) opening both ends and connecting them as a series of cylinders to become low-temperature ductwork for geothermal applications; (3) opening them all the way up flat and using the reflective metallic surface as a solar concentrator or mirror to deflect unwanted solar radiation away from buildings; or (4) my personal favorite, rolling them into a series of flat spirals to become electrical capacitors.[11]

---

[11] Author's side note: Serenity Noell, come back to me, finish your degree, and energy tech may continue to be!

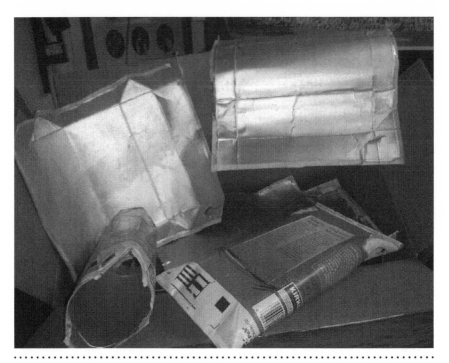

FIGURE 3.5. Photo of TetraPak bags. The one in the bottom right could become a bioreactor, and the cylindrical one in the lower left could become a low-temperature duct, whereas the upper two with their aluminum layers become reflective surfaces or electric capacitors.

Residing in a place as remote as Missoula in the age of consumption means that an artifact's path from the lower right corner of the recycling triangle of Figure 2.2 back to its apex can be long and tortuous. This is especially true for glass bottles (Figure 3.6). In Missoula, the artistic and innovative hub that it is, that path can also manifest itself in many creative ways. For designers looking for that LEED touch, this can mean taking a durable artifact such as an entire wine bottle and turning it into a window[55]; transforming a water bottle for drinking or gardening into a greenhouse, as some Sentinel High School Students have done with plastic bottles; or creating concrete countertops[12] and building exteriors from pulverized glass (Figure 3.7).

One of my next goals is to build and market water catchment systems using old wine bottles (as shown in Figure 3.8). It is my sense and my hope

---

[12] http://stampinggroundstudios.com.

that this will catch on in a city obsessed with how to repurpose its used glass vessels.

FIGURE 3.6. Glass bottles amid other Missoula artifacts on their way back to the technosphere.

FIGURE 3.7. The Missoula Federal Credit Union Russell Street branch facade in Missoula is made of pulverized glass embedded in concrete.

FIGURE 3.8. Stay tuned for an embodiment of this water catchment system at a garden store or farmer's market near you.

Zero-Waste Challenges Met

One major conundrum in the plight to remain landfill-free is learning when to let go. Central to this is the notion "Oh, I'll finish that project later." I encounter this frequently, especially at the intersection of sustainable waste management and sustainable energy practices. Not too long ago, I had a student build a solar thermal air exchanger for my office on campus. To boost thermal efficiency, we insulated the heat exchanger. Without knowing just how hot it would get, we selected a polystyrene-based insulation, only to discover that, when the air exchanger approached 240 °F, the expanded polystyrene began to melt and off-gas, resulting in an odor that was not only offensive but potentially toxic[10,42,80,129,151]. To remedy the problem, we unmounted the air exchanger from my office; carefully vacuumed out all the polystyrene; replaced the insulating layer with fiberglass, which has a much higher melting temperature; and reinstalled it on a new home under construction (Figure 3.9), thus preserving the technology and putting it back into the technosphere, rather than in limbo.[13]

---

[13] The vacuumed PS fragments await their fate in a pyrolysis waste-to-energy unit currently under development.

Another little company worth looking into that has turned the challenge of an ever-growing number of shipping containers into a business opportunity is Montainer. This little firm in Missoula has made a name for itself taking worn-out shipping containers and turning them into clean, comfortable, microhomes. One of their homes that ended up in the Bay Area was recently featured in *Sunset* magazine. Another Missoula company, TRU-Home Montana is following suit.

FIGURE 3.9. The refurbished solar thermal panel now provides carbon emission-free heat to this home in Blackfoot, Montana. In its present configuration, the panel faces east, for morning heat. Eventually the entire house will be rotated so that the panel faces south.

At about the same time, we were cleaning house at my office, and we moved a large shower stall that I had converted to a water catchment tub. On the same day that my son and I were to take these technologies to a partner organization, a friend called and asked for my advice on how to dispose of a cartop carrier that she had inadvertently driven into her house while pulling into her garage. If you've ever done this, you know what I'm talking about. So here we are taking these technologies to a partner organization with a similar sustainability mind-set (Figure 3.10).

FIGURE 3.10. The author and his son with Boris, the 1982 truck who got his start building the Alaska pipeline. Now he spends his retirement years hauling repurposed artifacts and compostables on their way to their fates. The garage-impacted cartop carrier is sandwiched between the solar thermal air exchanger and the shower stall-turned-water-catchment container. The pink pants, hand-me-downs from a former friend, also remain in limbo en route to the fiber markets or perhaps the tailor.

While the solar thermal air exchanger serves our academic partners in Browning, Montana, the water catchment and broken cartop carrier await their fates. Recently, I was able to repurpose some of the hardware for the carrier into a latch for my shed (Figure 3.11).

FIGURE 3.11. One of the metal brackets from the cartop carrier now serves as a latch for the ramp door to my shed. Yet another example of upcycling.

Naysayers

Over the past year, I've been conducting informal interviews with my neighbors, my students, and my fellow Missoulians, asking them about their recycling habits and practices and about their feelings on the monetization of their waste streams.

Most responses fall into one of the following eight naysayer categories, each of which is cynical, self-defeating, or simply an example of economic stalemate:

1. "I want to recycle, but I can't afford two curbside services." In other words, "I'm not wealthy enough to recycle." One of my neighbors had subscribed to a local curbside recycling service, but paying for two separate services to stop by each week became economically unfeasible with the tight income of this neighbor, who reverted to the single-stream landfill service.

2. "I only have like eight pounds of trash. Why should I pay as much as my neighbor does who has that 250-pound can?" For a period

of a month or two, this neighbor and I conspired to be landfill-free. It was great. I got straw bales for my chickens, plastic lids to take to Ulta, animal fat for biofuel, and all kinds of other goodies. When I was in a hurry, which is typically the case, or out of town and couldn't keep up with the triage, she reverted to the landfill. Maintaining neighborhood networks is key to success.

3. "That's my trash! Don't touch it!" I actually had this happen to me when I lived in Havertown, Pennsylvania. This is understandable, as there could be sensitive legal documents in one's garbage. The solution to this is a waste-to-energy where this sensitive cellulose-based material is shredded, compacted, and sold as sustainable fuel or fiber.

4. "The problem with recycling in this small town is contamination. No one knows how to sort materials properly." Become part of the solution, my friend. Don't cop out. Be a leader, not a cynic.

5. "It's all goin' in the garbage anyway. Who would actually pay me to take my garbage away?" Unfortunately, I have witnessed blue bags, which customers pay extra for, being thrown right into the kraken's maw. So in some cases, the nays have it. However, with ubiquitous social media at our fingertips, these practices do not go unnoticed and will either lead to the demise or the reform of these monopolistic practices.

6. "Why would I give you money to take away my recycling if I know you're going to make money on it?" This goes back to the famous problem where Bob and Mary are approached by someone offering them fifty dollars with the following ground rules: Bob gets to decide how much he gets, and Mary gets to decide whether or not to accept Bob's decision. If she agrees, she gets whatever Bob doesn't want. If she does not agree, they both get nothing. I ran this little experiment in my Recycling Technology course, and to my surprise, one student was actually willing to allow another to take all the money. Relax, folks, it's a free market. Find the best sustainable service and subscribe to it.

7. "My landlord is paying for it." In this case, one of my neighbors, even though he was going out of his way to recycle, had no control over the fate of his waste. He and his landlord were actually paying

an extra recycling fee on top of their landfill service with the local owner of the landfill, but the landfill employees, receiving no compensation for efforts to divert materials from the landfill, frequently put recycling bags into the dump truck. This segues to the next naysayer category.

8. "I don't have enough time." I frequently hear this with other chores like dishwashing and clothes drying. There are much deeper implications here, specifically the fact that the average human has approximately twenty technoslaves, or approximately twenty times his or her own energy at his or her disposal. For example, as I write this, the lights are on in the room, my laptop is running, toilets are flushing, a car is cooling and radiating its heat to the garage, the fridge is running ... If I had to do all this work, I would need twenty of me constantly pedaling, pushing, and pumping away. This begs the question of what we can either live without or redesign completely while maintaining our comfort and surpassing contemporary standards.

Upcycling

The practice of upcycling is essentially the practice of taking an artifact, a group of similar artifacts, or a group of dissimilar artifacts, and creating another more valuable artifact. In other words, the sum is greater than its parts. I have been able to achieve this with a shed and a gate made almost entirely of salvaged lumber, much of it from author Richard Manning, carpenter Adam Kocsondy, and architect Jeffrey Crouch (Figure 3.12). Another project built from reclaimed materials serves as the north entrance to the backyard (Figure 3.13).

FIGURE 3.12. The shed in my backyard, with the exception of the shingles, was made from 100 percent reclaimed lumber. The double clamshell door on the left opens and serves as a ramp for moving saws and other tools in and out. The Hardibacker seen in the seven-panel montage came from Home Resource. One panel depicting a sun is complete, and three are being laid out to be decorated with ceramic fragments accumulated from years of broken dishes, bowls, and the like. The extension cord serves as a temporary power line as I lay the electric lines.

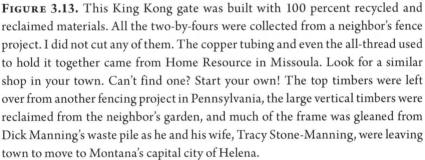

FIGURE 3.13. This King Kong gate was built with 100 percent recycled and reclaimed materials. All the two-by-fours were collected from a neighbor's fence project. I did not cut any of them. The copper tubing and even the all-thread used to hold it together came from Home Resource in Missoula. Look for a similar shop in your town. Can't find one? Start your own! The top timbers were left over from another fencing project in Pennsylvania, the large vertical timbers were reclaimed from the neighbor's garden, and much of the frame was gleaned from Dick Manning's waste pile as he and his wife, Tracy Stone-Manning, were leaving town to move to Montana's capital city of Helena.

There is likely no end to the number of ways that artifacts can be upcycled into larger artifacts. Of the "burn, bury, build" decision soon to be faced in chapter 5, "build" certainly takes the most time, ingenuity, and creativity.

In the Last Best Place, one particular artifact that there is no shortage of is the bottle cap. From what I have seen, bottle cap chain mail has yet to be invented and taken mainstream, but in a patent application I'm working on, I hope to create a stamping machine that pops six holes around the edge of a bottle cap, which are then threaded with discarded twist ties, or similar metallic wire artifact that would hold the caps together in a hexagonal lattice.

Exercises

1. Compare and contrast the hand ax relics to those that we are likely to leave behind today.

2. What will be the fates of the various artifacts that surround you right now? What should the salvage fee or salvage value be of each of these artifacts?

3. Do you have a curbside service? Is this more efficient than a drop-off service? Why or why not?

4. What do you estimate your own mass per day of waste to be? How much gets recycled? How much gets landfilled?

5. List a few things that you throw away that could stay in your own Land of YIMBY. List a few that you could easily give to your neighbors.

4

Materials

In Amory B. Lovins's 2011 book, *Reinventing Fire,* he writes that 98.98 percent of all materials extracted from nature on their way to becoming durable goods goes to waste[78]. I found this very difficult to believe at first, but I cannot think of a single example where I have been able to refute Lovins's calculations. That said, "waste" can take on a variety of meanings and definitions. One definition of waste is "matter that is not being used for its intended purpose."

Basics of Materials Triage

The first step in energy sustainability is conservation, rather than mindless deployment of renewable energy systems. The same holds true for material conservation. The first step in material sustainability is evaluation of whether or not a used artifact deserves to maintain its artifact status or be triaged to its material components.

As a case in point, on a recent bicycle ride home from work, I spotted the remnants of a garage sale left out on a table by the curb. A green fishing net with an aluminum frame sat there. It's in my garage now, and in perfect condition, not in the landfull. In addition to the aluminum handle and nylon net, a small plastic cap protects the open handle end. If the handle were bent, the net had a tear, or if the plastic cap were missing, the entire assembly would be less suitable as an artifact for catching fish. The nylon of the net, the aluminum of the handle, and the plastic cap all have scrap value of a few cents. As a new fishing net, you might find this for sale for ten to twenty dollars, but while out on the river with a giant fish on the line, the net is invaluable.

Thus the value in the artifact is a function of time and space, and it is the duty of the zee dubber to envision how best to facilitate the navigation of each artifact and chunk of matter through the space-time continuum as well as the real estate-finance continuum. How does one divert discarded items or streams of matter without diminishing the value of the place where it is stored en route to its next utilization? If you've ever watched the show *Hoarders*, you will understand the negative ramifications of taking waste diversion or collecting to the extreme. Some people featured on *Hoarders* have actually collected so much stuff that they are physically unable to move about freely within their own homes because they have created dangerous tripping hazards or even mounds of rotting food and feces. Others have been collecting discarded technologies such as cars and farm equipment for so long that they've created toxic soils on their own land. This is *not* a healthy way to live in the Land of YIMBY.

As someone who would rather see a technology such as the fishing net being put to use rather than aiding and abetting the further building of Mount Methane, I face this conundrum as well. Are the items and parts we saw in Figure 3.3 still artifacts, or are they better reduced to their material components?

Aluminum Cans

Aluminum cans (Figure 4.1) first became mainstream in the beverage industry in the 1940s and '50s following on the heels of the steel can. The manufacturing process has evolved from a pull top to snap top, thus saving beachgoers from countless stitches and blown-out flip-flops. This evolution has seen the evolution of the aluminum alloys used in beverage-grade cans and the constant trimming of the weight of the can as manufacturing tolerances improve.

On a recent trip to Japan, I was surprised to see the old, large flanged cans that went by the wayside in the United States in the 1980s. With their small size and thick walls, these cans might, in fact, be sturdy enough to sustain some serious structural loads. This would make for a challenging and rewarding project for anyone looking for an innovated sustainable living solution!

FIGURE 4.1. Japanese aluminum coffee cans. The beverages cost ¥100, or about $1, and emerge from vending machines nice and hot. As with many foods and beverages on the island nation of Japan, these coffees are brewed to perfection and a welcome antidote to jet lag. They also seem to be sturdy enough to build a tsunami wall!

Some philanthropic organizations have even provided an incentive for grade-school children to recycle by bringing in the pull-tops through charity organizations. Incidentally, this actually serves to purify the aluminum stream since the pull-top is a different alloy. My personal favorite use of the can itself is the solar thermal air exchanger we saw in chapter 3's "Zero-Waste Challenges Met" on page 34.

Plastic Bags

Ah, the ubiquitous plastic bag. Revered by Wal-Mart shoppers, banned in California. What could be handier than an infinite supply of nearly weightless membranes with built-in handles to tote your groceries and other goodies to your car or other means of conveyance on their way to your fridge or house? One goal while writing was to snag a photo of a bag that has been flailing in the wind in a tree near the Van Buren Street Bridge across the

Clark Fork River near the University of Montana's campus. However, while out and about one day on my Surly Steamroller with a big bunch of billowing plastic bags, I happened across a lone member of this invasive species in a little puddle out near "Big Box Avenue" in Missoula (Figure 4.2). Stuck in a puddle, the bag commands us to "Never Stop Improving." I immediately responded by stuffing him in with his cousins, and depositing them all into the bag return at Lowe's. Once small step for Mother Earth …

The plastic bag first emerged in the 1970s as an alternative to paper because of concern about forest loss or perhaps as an additional revenue stream for petroleum corporations or both, thus beginning the incessant question, "Paper or plastic?" This binary decision is being made hundreds of times per second and perhaps hundreds of millions of times per day across societies swamped in consumption. But is there a third option? How about "neither?" Foregoing the bag presents a conundrum since it is impractical to shop for mere armloads multiple times daily. For the waste-conscious, however, "neither" typically takes the form of the reusable canvas bag.

While giving my talk in Japan at Tohoku University on March 1, 2016, I had an audience member ask if I had heard of the recently developed technology that converts plastic to liquid hydrocarbons.[14] I had, and I know this technology will soon become commonplace. This liquefaction, however, does require heat, which may come from an electric source, which may come from a nonrenewable carbon-based fuel, furthering our climate conundrum. Once the liquid fuels have been produced, what shall be their fate? Most likely these liquid hydrocarbons will share the same fate as other ancient petrochemicals—the conversion directly into mechanical or thermal energy via combustion, et cetera, et cetera, et cetera …

---

[14] http://www.honestpyrolysis.com/index.php?id=product&cate=c3-1&pid=164.

FIGURE 4.2. Photo of plastic bag as discovered within a block of the Lowe's store in the Last Best Place. This bag was recovered as it was on its way to the Clark Fork River and, ultimately, the Pacific Ocean as I pedaled the Surly Steamroller with my Beast of Burden "BOB" trailer in tow through Big Box land. As fate would have it, I already had several stuffed bags of plastic and returned this rogue refined petroleum relic to a receptacle at the retailer of origin. After inquiring with the staff about procuring a contract to collect the Missoula Lowe's plastics, I was told that I would need to negotiate with "corporate."

If you follow any waste-stream news, you've probably heard of the gyres or islands of plastics in the ocean. While much of this is in the form of actual large plastic artifacts such as bags, gloves, bottles, toys, six-pack turtle-neck snaggers, and the like, the vast majority of it takes the form of microplastics, or small fragments of plastic shed from clothing or cars. And while most of us think, "Well I would never litter and throw something on the ground that would contaminate the ocean!" we're all guilty contributors.

Recently I was installing a webcam on Brennan's Wave in Missoula and realized that as I was sawing away on some PVC conduit, the tiny fragments that were coming from the hacksaw were going everywhere. They were landing on the observation deck, blowing in the wind, and would eventually make their way to the Clark Fork River and the Pacific Ocean. Once there, with their specific gravity of 0.98, or just 2 percent less than that of water, they would bob and swirl, until sunlight and saltwater eventually decomposed them back into elements 12 and 1, carbon and hydrogen, or in the case of PVC, some chloride, element 17.

But is degradation in the ocean really the ideal fate of the pervasive plastic plague? Certainly a less auspicious fate is the ingestion of the small particles by microscopic life, birds, or marine mammals such as whales.

And while I am not an expert on the health implications of plastic ingestion, scientific findings that reveal a beneficial outcome to ocean wildlife would be surprising.

Is it really possible, though, to keep all plastic fragments from finding their way to our oceans?

I learned from Stiv Wilson of the Story of Stuff Project during his April 2016 talk in Missoula that so-called microplastics in products such as toothpaste and sunscreen are now banned. This is good to know, I suppose. Perhaps this is a good example of a problem being solved in the health care and beauty product market before most of us were even aware that it existed.

While this ban on microplastics and the California ban on plastic bags will likely eliminate one tributary of the plastic streams heading to our oceans, it isn't likely we'll see the end of this flow unless things like tennis shoes, clothing, and most automobile parts are no longer made from petrochemicals. Where else will shoe bottoms go? Can we filter out all these little bits of hardy matter as they flow from our city streets, our highways, and our public places? Perhaps. Certainly cities with integrated storm water systems intercept much of it, but it's literally a race to the bottom if we are to divert all plastics and other nonbiodegradable materials away from the biosphere and back into the technosphere.

My own solution to the plastic that streams from 8 Columbine is to stuff grocery bags that find their way to my casa into an old spice rack that I've affixed to the ceiling (Figure 4.3). I then stuff them into a special bin at our local Albertson's grocery store, where they are baled and shipped back to corporate. But where do they go from here? Later in the book we'll discuss waste-to-energy solutions for plastic bags and other discarded artifacts made from polyethylenes.

FIGURE 4.3. Photo of plastic bag storage. An old spice rack serves as a spot to store plastic bags to be used to bale and recycle other #2 and #4 plastics common in food packaging.

Condoms, Rubber Gloves, Bicycle Tires, and the Like

Not too long ago, as I was sifting through the sundry matter in my garage, listening to the local college radio station, KBGA, I heard an old broadcast from WWII-era president Franklin Delano Roosevelt, asking that all Americans donate their "rubba."[15] "Send us your rubba!" FDR proclaimed and pleaded to his fellow Americans. Apparently during the war, access to rubber plantations was limited by the Japanese occupation, and there was a shortage of materials for making military vehicle tires. This put us into a recycling and even a carpooling frenzy.[16] Now that we're entering what might be thought of as a sustainability war with ourselves, does it not make sense to put those vulcanized disulfide bonds back into the technosphere? So send your condoms[17], rubber gloves, and other stretchy materials back

---

[15] http://www.learnnc.org/lp/editions/ww2-rationing/5911.

[16] http://www.learnnc.org/lp/editions/ww2-rationing/5914.

[17] Fortunately I have not had to bother with condoms since my vasectomy. Details on that ordeal in the next book …

upstream with your used tires (Figure 4.4). The whole mess will "be near a fire"[18] again soon.

Look around you. All the rubbers and plastics, and certainly all the metals you see in your built environment, have indeed been near a fire. This heat signature is yet another cost of civilization[112].

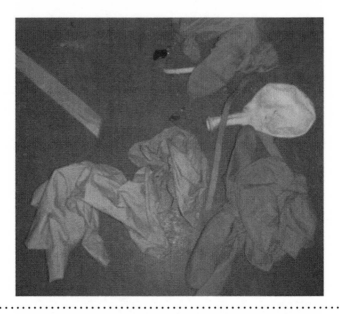

FIGURE 4.4. Rubber gloves, balloons, rubber bands, and other stretchy polymers should be sent to the same recycling centers as rubber automobile and bicycle tires where they may reenter the technosphere rather than being left to smolder in Mount Methane.

Fabrics

As you've gathered by now, a key to zero waste is to strive to sort materials into streams of similar materials. Fabrics are no exception. There is a market for every single material imaginable. To borrow a phrase of wisdom from the 1980s band Depeche Mode, "Everything counts in large amounts." So rather than flicking bits of fabric into "the garbage" or "the trash," send them back upstream to the technosphere to be repurposed as new fabric,

---

[18] This was a phrase my father-in-law frequently uttered during dinner when an unexpectedly hot dish arrived at the table.

insulation, mattress filler, sofa cushions, or other artifacts, where aesthetics are not a priority. For example, take your plastic bags back to the grocery store for baling. Take your glass bottles back to the store where you bought your beverages. Take your unwanted clothing to the secondhand stores, and take your outdated electronics back to the store where you purchased them. Don't be a naysayer expecting financial return for your temporal investment. You are paying the seventh generation forward.

Another key to successful fabric triage, as with most other material triage, is having a little patience, time, and space. I typically push all discarded smaller fabrics through a chute in the wall between my dining room and garage (Figure 4.5). Having this little portal from the living space into the outer realms of the household eliminates clutter from domestic life. Who wants to have dinner guests over to gaze over one's pile of recyclables? The next step in this evolution is to develop an integrated multistream system to minimize materials handling by the homeowner and move toward a touch-it-once model.

FIGURE 4.5. All midsize food-free artifacts and materials exit the interior of 8 Columbine by way of the six French waiters who hang on a hook above a six-by-fourteen-inch chute between the dining room and the garage.

Once materials have made their way through the magic chute to ground zero, they are then triaged by material type. For fabrics, I use a "disposable" garment or linen bag to stuff all fabric scraps into (Figure 4.6). This bag then makes its way back to Goodwill along with other clothing and donation artifacts.

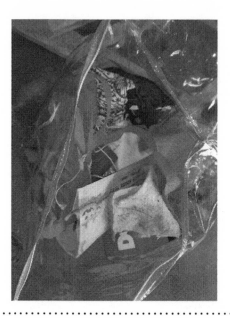

FIGURE 4.6. Various fabrics accumulating in disposable garment bag en route to Goodwill. I have yet to investigate the fate of fabrics that go unpurchased from my local Goodwill, but even a brief online tour of global fabric prices (chapter 10), especially coated fabrics (clothing and awnings) reveals a strong future demand.

Detritus

While cheap (free) plastic bags are typically used to carry the "goods," expensive (two- to ten-dollar) HEPA filter bags are typically used to carry the "bads." These engineered barriers between the debris we suck up off our floors and the air we breathe then become liabilities (Figure 4.7) that are typically bound for the landfill. My strategy has been to exhume the contents (Figure 4.8) into my non-gardening compost pile, let nature do the sorting, and then spread the bounty on the lawn. I'm certain that the diamonds that find themselves ejected from wedding bands are waiting patiently within these entropic heaps of domestic detritus.

FIGURE 4.7. Ah, the charm of domestic life. How far we have strayed from The Garden. But what compriseth the contents of this clever container?

FIGURE 4.8. Upon closer inspection of the vacuum bag, I found it to be comprised of what appeared to be pure dog hair. This keratin-rich substance is now turning to soil in the non-gardening compost pile. The bag itself awaits its waste-to-energy fate via a pyrolysis system my colleagues and I are developing.

At this point in the book, as we discuss materials triage, I want to reemphasize the practice of keeping like materials with like. For example, one common practice seen daily in the Last Best Place is that of using a plastic bag to pick up dog poop, carry it to a trash can, and send it to the landfill. This propagates the unnecessary manufacturing of single-use plastic bags, fails to squeeze remaining bioenergy from animal waste, and perpetuates the use of fossil fuel-burning garbage trucks. A solution to this underutilization has already been developed in the United Kingdom, where the Park Spark Project turns the methane effluent from animal waste into carbon dioxide and light. The poop itself is still picked up of course, but with a biodegradable bag.

For domestic cat waste, a biodegradable product known as Sweetscoop has been developed to mask odor and perform the essential act of clumping. By avoiding the mixing of petroleum-based polymers with biomaterials in the first place, we can move more quickly toward zero waste.[19] Our family previously used conventional cat litter to keep our kitty, Aleister Moody, tidy. At the time, I wasn't sure what constituted these popular brands of kitty litter. After a little research, and a year or two of composting it, I was relieved to find that conventional kitty litter is merely a type of mined clay. In the non-gardening compost pile, this clay becomes a muddy mush. "Ashes to ashes and mush to mush!" With the installation of the pet door, Aleister Moody now relieves himself behind various landscaping shrubs in the neighborhood. Why cats are more discrete with their defecation habits than dogs may have something to do with their vulnerability while assuming the position. Regardless, I do still have a little bit of cat litter hanging around near the foundation of the shed, in case the cat gets nostalgic for that old-fashioned ritual (Figure 4.9).

As alluded to, I have two separate composting systems. One gardening pile is for leaves, soil, lawn clippings, and other biomaterials that you wouldn't be horrified to see children playing in. The other non-gardening

---

[19] Occasionally, one of my neighbors who is not in the practice of walking her dog will collect the better part of a five-gallon bucket of dog doo from her front yard. She'll give it to me, and I'll simply lift the manhole (no need to be PC here) cover on my property line and send it downstream to our wastewater treatment facility. This is a temporary solution while we await the Park Spark Project to arrive in the Last Best Place.

pile receives all the rakings from the yard that appear at the end of the winter, including dog poop, deer droppings, and bear scat. It also gets all the wet compost from the kitchen, including coffee grounds, facial tissues, soiled paper towels, banana peels, avocado peels, biodegradable tampons, animal bones, and other materials that you *would* be horrified to see your children playing in. Once mature, this compost goes back on the ground as fill for neighboring lawns. For more details, check out the online version of the April 2016 issue of *Missoula* Valley Lifestyles Magazine[20].

FIGURE 4.9. A bit of cat litter remains amid the sawdust and other organic detritus near the foundation of my shed.

Exercises

1. Go to *Wikipedia* and find the resource for "embodied energy." (a) List the embodied energy of several materials in the units of MJ/kg. (b) Find the entry for photovoltaic cells and convert MJ/m^2 to MJ/m^3, using 300 μm as a typical thickness and compare to other common building materials such as concrete and polystyrene. (c) Using 4.4 hours of daylight at 1,000 W/m^2, calculate the number

---

[20] http://www.missoulavalleylifestyle.com/2016/03/28/leading-by-example

of days until the panels harvest more primary energy than it took to create them. (d) Do the same for a system using natural gas. How long until the natural gas harvests more energy than it took to create?

Solution:

metric with units	value
EE (MJ/m^2)	4000
thickness (μm)	300
layers per m^3	3,333
EE per m^3 (MJ)	13,333,333
m^3/m^2	0.0003
$kWh/m^2/day$	4.4
$MJ/m^2/day$	15.84
days to payback	253
months to payback	8.4
years to payback	0.69

2. Go online and Google prices for (a) bulk rubber, (b) bulk cotton, (c) shredded polyethylene, (d) post-consumer leather, (e) nylon, and (f) shredded polyester. Compare the prices to other commodities such as food and clothing on a per-pound basis.

3. Research the mining strategies for producing cat litter. Make an estimate of the fuel used to run the equipment to mine the minerals used in cat litter. Now look at the embodied energy in cat litter and do a carbon footprint analysis on putting the cat litter mineral back into the land once it has been mixed with cat feces.

5

Best Practices

In my ruminations on how best to distill the overall philosophy of zero waste into a slogan or mantra that might stick, I arrived at the 3B model—bury, burn, or build (Figure 5.1).

Fundamentally, these are the three inevitabilities—or fates, if you will—of all inanimate matter that is either (a) on its way *up* through some combustion process, (b) on its way *down* under the influence of gravity, or (c) *maintaining* its current elevation as part of our global technosphere.

As matter flows through my own sphere of direct physical contact, I attempt to glean as much utility from each given piece of matter as possible before sending it on its way. This may mean putting a Popsicle stick into a jar to be sent to the local art center, taking the time to compost a tissue, sweeping a broken bottle into a construction stream, or repurposing a webbed plastic bag into a dish scrubber. Perhaps the best way to visualize zero waste is to think of decelerating the flow around the recycling triangle we saw in chapter 2.

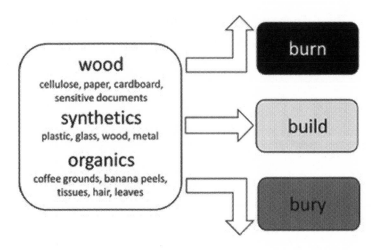

FIGURE 5.1. The principle of Occam's razor[21] applied to zero waste. All matter, regardless of whether the act is intentional or not, must either be on its way up (burn), down (bury), or somewhere in between (build). With this simple strategy, much of the head scratching is taken out of conventional household waste management.

But what does this model mean for things like biohazards that must be professionally handled or old toys, books, and appliances that have worn out their welcome? The key here is to harvest as much potential from the matter as it is flowing through your sphere of influence. But what does it mean to "add value" to something?

In the case of *burn*, the value added (extracted) is the heat or electricity. In the case of *bury*, valuable soil results from decomposing organic matter. For *build*, this means using materials at our fingertips to create new artifacts, which includes everything we see around us—dwellings, transportation infrastructure, manufacturing facilities, new energy technologies, and on and on[146].

But this approach now begs a question: Where is the *best place* to bury, burn, or build? In Montana, I've found it relatively straightforward to bury most of the biomass that flows through my yard and house directly in the Land of YIMBY. For the time being, I have been using typical biomass such as newspapers, spent paper towel rolls, soiled cardboard, and the like,

---

[21] Occam's razor is the philosophy whereby the most appropriate theory for any system should be as simple as possible, but not simpler.

in the fireplace. As for building, in addition to the practices described in the previous chapters, I continue to build the house with scrap materials, insulate with old fiberglass and dryer lint, plug little inconspicuous holes in the garage walls with chewing gum, and basically sequester tidbits of matter into the built environment (technosphere) that would otherwise burden the natural environment (biosphere).

Up to this point, we have begun to touch on some of the fundamental economics of space, matter, and time, but what about the monetary dimensions that underlie reality and permeate our societies? To the original three Bs we must now add a second trio of Bs.

In this more sophisticated (and more practical) triage model for the zero waster, we add buy, barter, and bank. For example, with various plastics selling for three to fifty cents a pound on global markets, one possible solution is to simply become a middleman in the global market and begin negotiations with local retail outlets such as those discussed in chapter 10. For those who already have day jobs, the best practice is to begin to get to know your community and your neighbors and come up with creative ways to share waste streams in such a way that, ultimately, every material and artifact makes its way back upstream or perhaps finds its way to a new economic oxbow to support a burgeoning industry in reclaimed materials.

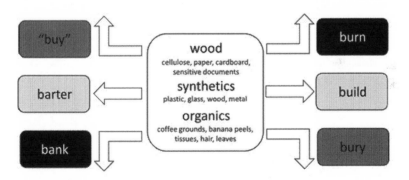

FIGURE 5.2. The economic side of the Occam's razor approach. All materials or artifacts that the recycler has in his or her possession can be sold (buy), traded (barter), or stored (bank).

Note the downsides of excessive banking, a.k.a. hoarding. The challenge for the zero-waste lifestyle thus becomes finding the appropriate socioeconomic network for triaging all the stuff that flows through one's sphere. Typically, those moving toward a zero-waste model will find that most of their post-consumer waste will flow out through the barter channel. This gray market yields no financial reward to the zee dubber, other than the avoidance of a landfill or recycling fee. The overall benefit to the general economy and to the environment is that things like spare paperclips, Lego sets, board games, furniture, and other used artifacts end up in the hands of those who can put them to use. This moves us away from the extraction, use, and dump economy toward an economy based more on creativity, revitalization, and sharing of information.

How To Do Triage at Home

Moving away from the trash can liner can be a little overwhelming at first. Just look at all the goodies these sacks of slop can sequester (Figure 5.3)! Inside this clean, white plastic sack are likely paper plates, bits of food, yard waste, tissue papers, and all the other dubious delicacies that flow from our domiciles.

The black trash bag, perhaps even more so than the white trash bag, is a cloaking device that allows us to mask our eyes from our waste as it is heading "away." The garbage bag, regardless of the color, allows for the mixing of the technosphere and the biosphere into a black hole of mounting stench that must be quickly moved to the curb, compressed to an even greater density, and then piled into a heap devoid of oxygen. Gravity then drives the process by creating increasingly dense layers, essentially mimicking the same physical and chemical processes that have given us our carbonaceous fossil fuels.

FIGURE 5.3. Photo of trash can on my "Green Blocks" street in Missoula, Montana. I did not triage this particular can, but in previous research, I have found coffee grounds, which should be buried; scraps of wood, like Popsicle sticks, which could be burned; and aluminum cans, which should be built with.

By swearing off the garbage can liner, be it black, white, or clear, we can clearly see and thus sort our waste streams into easily separable material and, ultimately, commodity streams. In fact, at the University of Montana, all recycling liners must be clear; otherwise, the contents are masked and, thus, unknown and bound for Mount Methane.

Food on the Plates

After meals, scrape your leftovers into the chicken bin or into the compost bin. Chickens love anything green—broccoli stalks, cucumber peels, pea shells, and bean shells. They also love to peck at corncob husks, pick up pieces of rice and bread crusts. Heck, chickens will indeed eat anything, so take care and watch what you give them. Green potato peels may be toxic to chickens in large quantities, and don't feed chicken meat to your chickens. That's just wrong. Give the leftovers from a chicken dinner to the dog, but save the bones for the fireplace or soil building.

Bones can pose a particular set of problems as there may be residual meat that could attract pests. I've made a practice of burying them deep in my compost or throwing them into the fire. Bones therefore sit at the boundary between *burn* and *bury*. If they take the *bury* route, they break down eventually and add valuable calcium to the soil. If they take the *burn* route, they produce a typical gas profile similar to burning wood. The ash will contain the same calcium and phosphorous and thus be safely returned to the soil.

Put things like avocado peels, banana peels, and other things you yourself wouldn't consider eating into the non-garden compost, along with animal waste and other topsoil. Keep this under the kitchen sink as a bucket without any holes in the bottom so that you can add fluids such as soggy coffee grounds to it as well. Compost piles need to stay wet to stay alive. By swirling out your coffee grounds, spent milk jugs, and moldy yogurt tubs into your compost, you'll help it stay warm and wet through hot dry summers and long cold winters in any climate. Compost piles come in numerous sizes and shapes, and we'll see much more from them in the next chapter, but I've discovered that the bigger they are, the more stable their temperature and moisture content become. Bigger piles also offer a more thorough exercise regimen and, of course, become a greater resource for amending neighborhood gardens and lawn soil.

Shower Time

The shower is a great place to take care of a lot of the business of cleaning in what might be called parallel-processing mode. For example, if I've been painting, working in the yard, or doing anything else that involves dirty rags, paintbrushes, and other such items, rather than putting these heavily soiled items in the washing machine and getting clothes dirty, I'll stop up the drain, hop into the shower, and stomp around a bit in the sloppy stew that ensues. You'll knock the topsoil off your feet and the rags. Hang them out to dry and then wash yourself clean. At the end of my shower, I typically wipe down the stall with my towel to reduce the humidity in the room that feeds mold and to keep calcium deposits off the fixtures.

Perhaps someday we'll get to the point where we have a biosphere sewer *and* a technosphere sewer, just as we have parallel systems for storm water runoff and sewage collection, but for now, all synthetic polymers such as latex that flake off from painting projects are relatively nontoxic. It's not clear what fraction of this microscopic inorganic material makes it through the screens and filters at a typical wastewater treatment facility, but the goal is zero toxic effluent back into our streams and eventually our oceans. Your municipal sewer system may take some or all its solids to the landfill, but many sewer systems are moving toward a waste-to-energy model, where the solids are gasified or pyrolyzed and converted to heat or electricity, rather than being shipped off in a nasty truck to an even nastier landfill.

Which category of burn, bury, or build does the wastewater being discharged from a treatment facility fall into? Depending on gas concentrations and chemical reactions occurring in the water, we should consider any off-gassing as burn, any solids that make their way to the river bed or ocean floor as bury, and the water itself as "build," as water is the physical structure that supports all aquatic life and, in fact, likely served as the physical matrix where the original building blocks of life assembled.

Laundry

Most modern American homes devote 5 to 10 percent of their energy budgets to clothes washing and drying. This practice of course generates a waste stream of heat, dirty water, and greenhouse gasses in the form of water vapor and carbon dioxide either at the appliance or the power plant. One way to minimize municipal water and energy waste is to wash clothes in a water stream collected directly from rainwater, rather than from water utility or well water, both of which likely rely on electricity-driven, and thereby carbon dioxide-generating, energy systems. To sustain hot water for clothes washing at home, a solar-thermal system fed by rainwater is one solution that avoids aquifer depletion and the acceleration of energy demands.

To create the mechanical agitation necessary to fully entropicize (mix) the suds with the clothes, a human-wind hybrid system that performs during stormy weather is the ideal low-energy solution. The wind is already blowing, and we humans need exercise. My students and I built such a human-powered clothes dryer system several years ago and found that simple line drying is more time-efficient. Putting wet things in a box to dry does seem counterintuitive, doesn't it? Another way to produce fossil fuel-free motive power is with a solar-driven Stirling engine. Stirling engines operate by creating pressure from solar radiation-derived heat, which is then used to move air and, thus, machinery.

Another future of distributed fossil fuel-free power that I envision running our appliances one day is a mechanical grid, whereby an interconnected set of driveshafts allows a network of nearby homes and businesses to supplement electromotive power to run a wide variety of appliances. This type of mechanical grid could also be used to store energy in existing water lines and tanks, further reducing the carbon-intensive practice of pumping water uphill with electricity. The bottom line on laundry is that there are solutions for heating water and mechanically agitating a slurry of soapy water and fabric that do not require the burning of fossil fuels or depletion of radioactive materials to generate electricity. Let's put some public and private funding into these solutions now for a diverse, sustainable clean future of energy and human health.

Landfill Negative

Lately I've been challenging myself to go beyond zero waste to the point of being landfill negative, a.k.a. dumpster diving. There are numerous artifacts around my home that I've gleaned from the garbage cans of my wealthier neighbors. This includes decorative baskets, lawn furniture, vacuum cleaners, holiday decorations, deck furniture, clothing, innumerable conventional recyclables, dog toys, tools, and even entire bicycles. All these items were en route to Mount Methane due to a perceived lack of time, combined with a true lack of information and communication among the various networks of those in need of the aforementioned artifacts.

As I stated in my recent interview with *Missoula Valley Lifest*yles, I do not disparage my neighbors for landfill habits. Rather, I look forward to the day where my fellow tribes people here in Missoula unite for a truly sustainable system of a zero-waste community. If successful, we will turn our multimillion-dollar annual landfill bill into a profitable source of revenue for the entire community. There really is no finger-pointing to be done here. We all do the best we can with what we have. The blame lies with all of us for not doing a better job making upstream decisions on what we purchase in the first place. The blame also lies within our society for lacking the entrepreneurial spirit to turn all trash into cash.

Street Cleaning

When I first moved to Missoula, my only vehicle was a Surly Big Dummy, one of the first production utility bikes of its kind. I made a special, wood-framed cardboard box for it and had it shipped from the Main Line just outside the City of Brotherly Love to the Last Best Place. Once in Missoula, I used the bike on a daily basis to bring tile saws, power drills, and other remodeling tools back and forth from a community tool share called MUD, or Missoula Urban Demonstration Project, to the place I was staying. These were some of the simplest and most productive days of my life. I thoroughly enjoyed the simplicity of exchanging work for rent, improving the house I was living in, and feeling good about being one less car owner.

Within a year or so, I had the notion to build a trailer for the Dummy, as I was beginning to exceed the five-hundred-pound payload capacity with some of my hauls. I used a wooden shipping pallet and a couple of twenty-inch wheels that had served my students well on previous American Society of Mechanical Engineering Human-Powered Vehicle Challenges. With this, I was able to haul an additional five hundred pounds of leaves (Figure 5.4). Looks like a scene from *How the Grinch Stole Christmas!* huh?

FIGURE 5.4. I'm not quite there yet, but one of the goals of this endeavor is to achieve 100 percent human power as a means of moving materials. With a two-inch ball hitch installed on my Surly Big Dummy and a trailer made from a shipping pallet, I was able to make soil with about seven hundred pounds of leaves, grass, and animal waste that otherwise would have been headed for Mount Methane. Why on earth, and I do mean quite literally *why on planet Earth*, in the Last Best Place, would we wrap God's green grass in the devil's black bags en route to an unholy Temple of Trash?

Fireplace

Until very recently, the fireplace represented the focal point of most modern homes (Figure 5.5). The fireplace connects us with our ancestors, who first mastered this fourth form of matter known as plasma tens of thousands of years ago. The fireplace at 8 Columbine is a massive structure built from eight-inch cinder blocks. It has three flues. One serves the upstairs, and another serves the downstairs. The third is sealed. My intention is to convert the entire stack into a carbon-negative system modeled after Craig Thomas's BioFilter Reactor and the Chemical Looping System under the direction of Anders Lyngfelt of the Chemical-Looping Combustion Laboratory at Chalmers University of Technology in Gothenberg, Sweden.

Another colleague in Missoula, Nathan Taylor—his company is called COBrew ("see-oh-brew")—is creating a system to capture carbon dioxide streams from breweries. With a particulate filter and a carbon sequestration system such as these, I hope to heat the home with sustainable biomass without further polluting the Rattlesnake Valley with particulates and, ultimately, to keep carbon dioxide from 8 Columbine and anywhere else such systems are being used from entering the atmosphere. In fact, integrating the sewer stack, the furnace stack, and the chimney stack into a single waste gas stream that is pumped into and filtered by the municipal sewer is the ultimate goal here. It is this type of innovation that I believe Ronald Bailey and his colleagues are relying on innovators to innovate so that their prognostications of continuous improvement of the human condition can be realized[5].

FIGURE 5.5. The humble family hearth. It's the burn leg of the zero-waste tripod. Woody biomass that fails to make it over the "build" bar feels the "burn" herein. An ash pit in the back moves noncombustibles toward the bury stream. Occasionally when we burn construction materials, metals find their way to the ash stream. Next on the agenda is an appropriate technology to bifurcate the ash stream toward the technosphere or biosphere.

Cat Closet

One issue we ran into having two pets was the disparity in their eating habits. One animal (the dog) will devour anything remotely edible immediately upon scent and sight, and another (the cat) seems to require a persistently nonempty bowl. With a cat-size hole cut into one of the closet shelves and some scrap carpeting stapled to the wall and shelf, we were able to satisfy kitty's propensity for climbing, while keeping his food out of the dog's reach (Figure 5.6).

Figure 5.6. As animal lovers, we were looking for a way to keep the cat's food accessible but out of reach of the dog. The solution was to cut a hole in a closet shelf, add some old carpeting to the wall for traction, and give the cat a peaceful place to dine.

Triaging Examples at Work

Let's say that by now you're experimenting with, or even committed to some of the practices that I've outlined in this book. You've done away with your trash can liners, you've put together a little starter compost pile, no more artifacts are on their way to the landfill, but now you're wondering how to pull off these quirky habits at work.

First of all, congratulations; you're on the road to contracting a zero-waste psychosis! Here are a couple of examples of how I've been able to take these practices to work, baffle my custodians, and keep my office mates entertained (only one citation from the fire marshal so far!). I, of course, began by taking the black high-density polyethylene (HDPE) garbage can liner out of the wastebasket in my office and bundling it with other thin film plastics. These are all now being baled at the University of Montana's Recycling Station under the expert direction of Recycling Director Extraordinaire Edi Stan. Once baled, these putrid pastries of petroleum will be given or sold to my colleague Patrick Browne's International Biomass Group to be converted into MountainPellet fuel.

With the can liner out of the way, my wastebasket is the perfect container for receiving coffee grounds (along with the coffee filter, as it is made from wood fiber). I also routinely encourage those with a dirty tissue to deposit them into the office compost. It can also accept any other food waste, as well as grounds-keeping waste. Once full, I take it home on the Surly Big Dummy and add it to the non-gardening compost pile, which eventually becomes topsoil.

Another way to coordinate your zero-waste efforts between home and office is to shuttle food that is nearing its expiration between the two locations. You *know* the best way to make the other half of that giant Costco pie or birthday cake disappear is to simply put it out on the table in the break room. Pizza left over from an office party makes for a great weekend snack or meal too!

Chickens

One of the true pleasures of my day is walking out in the snow or the frost or the dew of the morning and giving Sunny and Rose their daily meal of chicken scraps (Figure 5.7). We keep a separate little tub on the kitchen counter that receives lettuce stubs, cucumber peels, burned rice, uneaten oatmeal, popcorn kernels, and occasionally some expired seafood—basically anything that you might consider eating if you were a little hungrier or if the timing had been a little better. Sunny and Rose are now in their fourth year and have been laying eggs faithfully all their lives. We also supplement these scraps with chicken feed, which runs about fifty cents a pound.

Another backyard pleasure is pitchforking through some mature compost. Here one finds some of the biggest, juiciest (or so I'm told) earthworms you'll ever see in North America. The Pavlovian response from the old birds is fantastic as well. The sight of these two feathered reptile descendants darting for a sluggish annelid never dulls. Another strategy for ensuring these hens get plenty of protein, and maybe even some chitin, is to simply roll over a log that sits at the boundary of the compost. This typically reveals the pill bugs and centipedes that thrive in this nether region. It's somewhat of a rapid and brutal end, being snatched from one's habitat into the gullet of a chicken, but such is the web of life in the Land of YIMBY.

FIGURE 5.7. Rose and Sunny on the prowl for bugs. Yes, it's true. Chickens will eat absolutely anything. This makes for a special challenge during construction projects, when bits of insulation and fragments of metal tend to find their way to the ground. So keep it clean, America!

The coop itself (Figure 5.8) I fabricated from lumber I scored from none other than Richard Manning. Dick approached me in 2012, asking if I might be able to put some of his old lumber to use. This is the equivalent of asking one of the free-living folks of downtown Missoula if they might have a use for a bottle of Jack Daniels. Upon my affirmative answer, Dick promptly fetched Boris (Figure 3.10), and we nimbly moved his accumulation of odd-shaped lumber from under his garage to my north-side pile. The coop was thus hatched. As we performed our scrap wood transferring task, Dick offered a little story behind each piece of lumber. One such hand-hewn piece came from a local elm tree that was either ill or unwanted. Fittingly, the coop now serves as a temporary storage location for wood gleaned from another neighbor who recently moved. The fate of this fresh delivery remains to be determined.

FIGURE 5.8. Chicken Coop. The materials for this coop were free—the boards were hand-me-downs from Dick and Tracy Stone-Manning's move from Missoula to Helena. In the photo, the recently acquired wood from the carpenter neighbor who just moved out obscures the view of Dick's hand-hewn elm. Stop by 8 Columbine any time to see it in person. Several people already have!

Time Capsuling

Shanta and I once went to a time capsule opening at Burns Park Elementary School in Ann Arbor, Michigan. The event was to be held at the turn of the millennium, which it was. I even managed to save the invitation, which is now over forty years old and will likely be time capsuled itself (Figure 5.9). When we went to dig up this alleged ancient urn with Shanta's grade school classmates, it eluded us. We looked in every corner under the stage in the auditorium and even dug a large hole atop a mound of dirt in the middle of the playground—to no avail. Perhaps some future generation will stumble upon it, or maybe it's sitting in a landfill near Ann Arbor. Regardless, time capsuling is a means of keeping small sentimental stuff that you cherish but don't have the bandwidth to ogle or fondle every day in a state of limbo. This practice fills space, builds memories, and serves as a portal to the past.

FIGURE 5.9. Photo of time capsule invitation. How far in the future the year 2000 seemed in 1974! There's a decent chance that this capsule remains to be discovered there at Burns Park School!

Consciously or not, we are all constantly creating our own time capsules. What will your house look like when you die? What's in the glove box of your car? What kind of junk lurks in other storage you may have? Over the past couple years, I've been using the wall that I'm building in the backyard as a time capsule of sorts. The wall itself has been fed a diet of old incandescent lightbulbs, bits of broken windowpane glass, dustpan contents, and other sundry inorganic material (Figure 5.10).

The two metal posts have been receiving other little nibblets of domestic life, such as spare board game pieces, toy army men, an occasional aluminum gum wrapper, a cigarette butt or two, and other stuff that has minimal chance of reentering the biosphere, since the posts are buried three feet into their four-foot concrete footers. Maybe we'll convert them into gasifiers at some point and harvest the chemical energy buried in the organic bonds and then send the nonreactive remains to another build project.

FIGURE 5.10. The two metal posts of this wall under construction are time capsuling much of the smaller bits of detritus that ebb and flow through the typical suburban home. The wall itself is also sequestering inorganic matter with no other purpose than occupying space.

When I try to categorize time capsuling into the burn, bury, build model, I can't help but think of Richard Feynman's now famous 1959 "Plenty of Room at the Bottom" talk and subsequent 1984 talk entitled "Tiny Machines." This talk ushered in the nanotechnology era. I'm also reminded of the middens left by our ancestors of the San Juan Islands off northern Washington State, "The First Ones."

As I learned from Ted Carns's philosophy on zero waste, there is not a one-size-fits-all solution. As you build your own Land of YIMBY, I look forward to hearing of your creative solutions.

Exercises

1. What does your default time capsule look like now? What should you get rid of so that others do not have to?

2. What can you turn into a scrapbook that you would be proud of?
3. Do you have any old art to frame and sell? What about any old artifacts that you could make money on right now?
4. See if you have a friend who does decoupage art. He or she is probably looking for discarded materials to turn into artwork.

6

Compost

One of the most curious practices I've witnessed is the seeding, watering, fertilizing, mowing, raking, bagging, and landfilling of invasive grass species with the use of imported seeds, water pumped from the Missoula aquifer using coal-fired electricity, salts distilled from petrochemicals, gasoline-powered lawnmowers, and petrochemical-derived black plastic bags that are then driven by petrochemical-fueled trucks to the top of a growing pile of methane-belching sludge. Yee-haw! I can hear that Saturday and Sunday suburban symphony playing now!

In an attempt to make 8 Columbine Road a net-positive soil producer, I have been using human power to divert the waste from this obscene practice into my own yard. With a Surly Big Dummy, its five hundred-pound payload, and a wooden pallet that I salvaged from a photovoltaic panel I purchased, I am able to intercept this biomass encased in its petrochemical mask, thus separating the technosphere from the biosphere. Remember Figure 5.4? YIMBY in action, my friends! These leaves, grass, pine needles, rocks, sand, dirt, and animal wastes are now being churned, mixed, eaten, and converted into soil on what is otherwise becoming a barren landscape in some frivolous competition to keep up with the Joneses.

Beyond the challenges of seeing our neighbors needlessly sending biomass to the landfill, I personally have a challenge seeing driftwood and sunken timbers clogging the beautiful waterways of the Pacific Northwest. So one fine day a few years ago, I gave myself the personal challenge of hauling a decorative piece of driftwood back to the ranch. I did this with an eighteen-volt cordless DeWalt drill, a two-inch Forstner bit, and a kayak cart.

I used the same two-inch ball hitch that I had installed on the Big Dummy and brought this beauty home. You'll see this in Figure 9.5 on page 120.

According to popular statistics, one-third of food, or approximately four hundred billion dollars of edible food per year, is wasted worldwide. That sounds like a lot, but is it? Turns out it's just the equivalent of each of us going to the grocery store, buying fifty-four dollars in food per year and sending it to the landfill. It's not clear how a dollar value can truly be placed on food, since all individuals value dollars to vastly varying degrees. Nevertheless, even the Pope is in on the action. He recently declared food waste *a sin*[46].

There are many other institutions addressing this issue. For example, Missoula Food Bank will accept donations from other entities in town with leftovers. A student group in Sweden has developed a process for preserving food as a powder they call FoPo that is beginning to address the gap between food waste and hunger.[22] As a case in point, as I write this, I'm in the process of spending twenty dollars plus on a Cobb salad and a beer at an airport restaurant, which is more money than most people will earn in a month. Nevertheless, hunger and starvation is not a shortage issue but a logistics issue to be solved, with money itself serving as no more than a lubricant for moving edible materials toward hungry mouths.

Composting Basics

In keeping with the 3B model, composting is essentially burying biology. It effectively gives material that has crossed into the human realm, which is poised between the technosphere and the biosphere, an immediate return path to nature in a backyard or other commons area. In fact, many cities, such as San Francisco, have banned the sending of organic material to the landfill [119].

In our kitchen, we separate food waste into two streams—one for the chickens and one for direct composting (Figure 6.1).

---

[22] http://m.huffpost.com/us/entry/55a7f337e4b0896514d09de1.

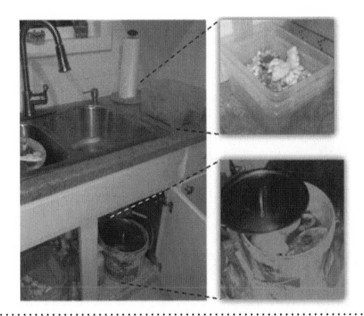

FIGURE 6.1. Kitchen sink composting system. Our container for the chickens is on the counter to the right of the sink. The compost container, an old three-gallon paint bucket, is below. The rule of thumb for the chickens is that they'll eat anything we would eat if we were just a bit hungrier. The chickens also get their own eggshells for a calcium boost. The compost bin gets things like coffee grounds, banana peels, and other cellulose-based materials like napkins. Other natural fibers like cotton also end up here en route to becoming soil.

The chickens grind through the cucumber peels, broccoli stalks, melon rinds, and any other vegetable scraps that have not been treated with pesticides. They also tear through any meaty leftovers that missed their opportunity at human consumption. This is usually a result of our inattention to leftovers in the fridge. We crush their leftover eggshells as well, to keep the calcium in their diets. As I said, we don't feed them actual chicken meat or chicken eggs; that's just wrong. Chicken meat scraps and any uneaten egg scraps go to the dog.

Scraps like banana and citrus peels head to the non-gardening southwest compost pile (Figure 6.2), where the toxic pesticides and herbicides are broken down thermally and biologically. This pile has become rife with centipedes, pill bugs, and gigantic earthworms. We've yet to see any bears or raccoons invade, as we always bury the waste from the three-gallon bucket at least two feet with the posthole digger and cover it over with nearby soil or compost, thus dispelling the often quoted "You can't compost in the Rattlesnake Valley."

FIGURE 6.2. Southwest non-gardening compost. Photo courtesy of *Missoula Valley Lifestyles Magazine* photographer Lisa Hensley, Details Photography. The two yellow handles belong to the posthole digger, which allows fresh kitchen scraps to be sequestered deeply enough to prevent varmint invasion.

This pile also receives any yard waste that might have dog droppings or other things that you might not want in your vegetable garden. After sitting for a couple of years, this rich medley makes great topsoil. Just this year, we donated five or six wheelbarrows full to neighbor Nick, who had the misfortune of a water main break. The crew that replaced his line left a muddy six-inch-by-two-foot trench in the yard, which we filled and is now part of the lawn (Figure 6.3).

Previously in Missoula, the water utility was privately owned. If a service line between the main and the curb ruptured, it was the homeowner's responsibility to pay for the repairs. In the case of neighbor Nick's lawn, after the repairs had been made to the pipe, the regrading of the soil was done hastily and unprofessionally, leaving a significant swale in the yard. This was the perfect opportunity to put some compost from the southwest pile to work locally. As can clearly be seen in Figure 6.3, the soil amendment coming from my pile is much darker and carbon-rich than the surrounding soil, which receives a salt-based fertilizer. The deeper green indicates greater access to sustained nitrogen than the ammonia-based fertilizers provide. Keeping organic material out of the landfill through the practice of composting is one more way that we can improve our nation's soil security[2].

FIGURE 6.3. Neighbor's yard shortly after a treatment of compost from the non-gardening southwest pile. Note the deep black color of the soil. The grass is greener too!

Bears, Deer, and Raccoons

In Montana, a common concern that rural and urban neighbors share is that of bears being attracted by their compost piles. As alluded to above, this is frequently a deal breaker for even the most ardent conservationist. Our approach to this threat in the Land of YIMBY is twofold. First, we use a posthole digger to auger out a hole that has about twice the volume of a typical compost load. Our bucket (Figure 6.1) holds about three gallons, so four or five good digs with the posthole digger makes a fine hole. Next, we dump the load in, fill in over it with topsoil or other mature compost, and then cover it with a black vinyl tarp. The tarp itself serves the twofold purpose of maintaining moisture and heat, both of which are a particular challenge in our cool, arid climate.

We also live in a neighborhood with a covenant from the late 1960s. It calls for low, transparent fencing of the chain-link or split rail variety or a hedge no taller than four feet. None of these three solutions is sufficient to prevent bear intrusion. Most chain-link fences in the neighborhood bear the marks of lost bear battles. Bent gates no longer close properly, top rails have become disconnected form their receivers, and chunks of fence dangle from their clasps.

Since putting in a higher fence is not allowed, we opted for more of a screen to keep deer from decimating the garden. The screen is made from black plastic netting or, in some places, black plastic-coated wire. It's dark and fine enough to be visually unobtrusive but stout enough to hold the deer at bay for the most part. Unlike our former trash-barreling selves, we've yet to have a bear breach, which I interpret as a complete absence of any easily accessible food waste and a general lack of temptation from the compost. Apples, plums, and pear trees that decorate the neighborhood are far more tempting and nutritious!

Sadly, we have had a few raccoon encounters, one of which resulted in the loss of Tulip the chicken and another where we lost a little clutch of chicks too, due to an improperly stapled bit of chicken wire. But such is life at the wildlife-urban interface (WUI) in the Wild West.

Cucumber Seeds

During a recent meeting with the zero-waste subcommittee of the Zootown Climate Smart Initiative, I had the good fortune to finally meet a man about whom I had heard several bits of good local lore. Mark Vander Meer is a Missoula icon who is known for his use of reclaimed lumber. He allegedly has a very green thumb as well. When I was discussing my composting practices with him and expressing my concern over some of the things that were going into my pile, such as paper plates, napkins, and the occasional dog turd, he suggested that I use cucumber seeds as a canary in the coal mine. Cucumber seeds, he said, are particularly susceptible to toxins; if they could thrive in the soil, then I had little to worry about. We promptly planted a small cucumber plant in a pot of soil from the back compost pile, and it is doing fine. As of this writing, it has been eaten, and portions of the chemical energy gleaned from it are likely assisting in the composition of this book.

Mowing

As I write this particular section of this book on a cool Montana summer morning, I'm watching a six-bladed lawn mower rip across the outdoor swimming pool parking lot to reduce four-inch blades of grass to two-inch blades of grass. To perform this act of landscape manicuring, (1) long-chain carbon molecules that were sequestered millions of years ago were sucked to Earth's surface and (2) trucked or piped to a refinery, where they were (3) boiled and separated in a thermal frenzy. They were then (4) driven to a filling station, (5) pumped into a gasoline can, (6) poured into the tank of the mower, (7) pumped to the mower's combustion chamber, and (8) squeezed together with oxygen molecules that themselves may be millions of years old to (9) create a miniature explosion in order to (10) push a piston to (11) turn a camshaft to (12) drive a mower blade in a circle—to whack the leaves of grass to a uniform height.

This convoluted path from brontosaurus booty to bocce field is of course practiced for the production of lush, green, grassy surfaces on which to kick a ball around or knock a golf ball back and forth or just plain admire. In the end, we're left with some short grass for a few days and a hotter atmosphere. What is the efficiency of this strategy versus using a reel mower pushed with human power? While the *time* spent driving the gasoline mower is five to ten times less than that of relying on human power, the *efficiency* of using ancient biomass (oil) to manicure recent biomass (grass) is on the order of one ten thousandth of a percent (0.0001 percent). To put this into perspective, we are currently drawing from ancient carbon banks ten million times faster than nature created them[23]. Sustain that, brontosaurus breath!

So besides mowing to make sports fields fairer, what motivates us to be urban grass farmers? Why do we continue to devote fossil fuel consumption

---

[23] https://www.youtube.com/watch?v=RKfgZ4Gu16o&t=90s

and carbon dioxide pollution to cut through purposefully planted landscaped vegetation? When we mow our lawns with gasoline-powered mowers or even electric mowers, we convert carbon bonds that were formed by solar-driven photosynthetic nanomachines millions of years ago into greenhouse gassing carbon dioxide. The mower comes along thwacking away at the leaves of grass, rereleasing carbon dioxide molecules, creating noise and millions of little grass clippings. Wherein lies the utility? Why do we persist with this practice? The answer likely dwells within relatively recent DNA that helped us avoid being eaten by very large cats who hid in tall grass prior to pouncing. To take care of those ungainly grass blades, let's hire the next generation of engineers to build silent, solar-powered, self-guided mowers to run on Saturdays while we polish the bocce balls for a serene Sunday game.

During a recent summer Energy Technology Practicum, I was walking across campus with a student from the Blackfeet Tribe and commenting to her about how much water from the sprinklers was pouring onto the sidewalks, parking lots, and simply running back into the storm drain without serving its intended purpose. She responded by saying, "But you need the grass to be green so that people will want to come to school here." I know she said this in all seriousness, but it made me question the effects our Western European culture has had on her and her ancient culture of waste not, want not.

Personally, I would much rather see a natural landscape or a food-cultivated landscape than the dandelion- and crabgrass-infested chemical green that seems to appeal to the masses. Individuals who have stepped away from this include Heather Jo Flores, author of *Food Not Lawns*[43], and Sarah Baker of Ohio, who was recently interviewed[24] on National Public Radio for her stance against the putting-green lawn. Public opinion is not likely to change as long as there are discrepancies in incomes and values, which of course will persist. In a familiar paradox, wealthy people spend money to stay slender in our age of plenty, while poor people purchase calorie-laden starchy and sugary fast foods. In a similar irony, wealthy people, or those wishing to appear so, will also spend money on sprinkler systems, fertilizer, and lawn care while the disadvantaged breathe the fumes and dust clouds formed by two-stroke engines and leaf blowers.

---

[24] http://www.npr.org/2015/08/05/429774004/mowing-the-law-giving-you-hard-time-let-it-grow

Topsoil

As we just saw, the spoils of the kitchen, garden, and yard are easily returned to the earth. Why then would the facilities staff at the University of Montana put actual topsoil into a dumpster en route to Mount Methane (Figure 6.4)? The reason lies in the same financial reason that people take longer showers when on vacation and the bill has already been paid.

FIGURE 6.4. Photograph of sod in the dumpster behind the Art School at the University of Montana. Also seen in the dumpster is a paper cup and a few plastic bags. What could the excuse be for throwing away topsoil?

Clearly we can do better as a campus whose leadership set the goal of being carbon neutral by 2020 and as evidenced by the other multiple compost piles on campus and by the pile at the PEAS Farm, a campus affiliate in the Rattlesnake Valley. The calculations that I've performed in my Recycling Technology Course indicate that the University of Montana can eliminate our four-hundred-thousand-dollar-per-year landfill bill and turn our waste stream into a one-million-dollar-per-year income stream, which would help a campus recently battered by declining enrollment.

Exercises

1. What might you put in the compost pile that you previously did not?
2. If you don't have a compost pile, make a list of neighbors nearby who might want to start one with you. Contact them this weekend.
3. Where might you use your compost once you've made it? Inside? Outside?
4. List the obstacles to composting and a set of solutions for moving beyond them.

7

Landfill

You the reader are likely a person like me who questions, perhaps even abhors, waste. And if you are also a person who is compelled to do the right thing, you likely question why others don't see the world the same way you do.

As of this writing, the public does not own the property just north of Interstate 90 on the north edge of Missoula that is the site of the regional landfill (Figures 1.7 and 7.1). Republic Services, the second-largest nonhazardous solid waste management company in the United States, does. For about a dollar per day, Republic drives a rig similar to that depicted in Figure 1.5 right up to the end of your driveway and puts anything and everything that you stick inside a black bag at the top of the landfill that they own. Here, birds and other wildlife feast upon our refuse as we pile it up at a rate of seven pounds per person per day—and contribute to Republic's annual revenue of $8.8 billion. With nearly a hundred thousand subscribers to the Missoula landfill alone, that's seven hundred thousand pounds per day, or nearly one hundred thousand gallons, or approximately one Olympic swimming pool every week or two. At that rate, Missoula will be able to build an Empire State building of garbage every couple of years. This is pointless behavior, yet we willingly participate daily.

I have a colleague and friend who leads the zero-waste team at a local reclamation and upcycling operation here in Missoula known as Home Resource. He and I have had several philosophical discussions regarding whether or not waste is inevitable. In fact, we took this debate public when we recently collaborated with the City of Missoula in declaring its intent to work toward becoming a zero-waste community (formally declared by Missoula mayor John Engen in a March 2015 proclamation). In it, we proclaimed that "waste is not inevitable." Upon closer scrutiny, however, it appears as if the converse is true. In all dynamic systems, matter and energy flow in and out. The third law of thermodynamics dictates that no system is truly at rest. Energy transfer happens, as does material transfer.

The stuff flowing out must then be viewed as either waste or product. Perhaps the philosophy by which my associate and I can both win our argument is to concede that matter does indeed flow through systems and that it's up to the ecosystem in question to find a use for the matter that is not part of the product. Either way, the fact that humans create landfills (Figure 7.1) is not up for debate. The scar upon the earth in the figure can be healed. Let's transform this area into a materials recovery facility, bundle the materials, and keep them building the economy, rather than a nasty pile for future generations to contend with. Let's all become participants in the emerging zero-waste economy.

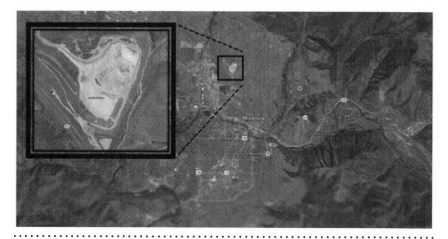

FIGURE 7.1. Google Earth image of Missoula's landfill, a.k.a. Mount Methane, which is privately owned by Republic Services. Is this really the best we can do? As of this writing, the landfill occupies a piece of real estate larger than the entire University of Montana's campus and is twenty to thirty stories high, with a specific gravity that is two to three times greater than water[150]. Are we not at risk of turning the Last Best Place into a lunar landscape[113]?

Landfills are essentially the modern version of the famed middens of the San Juan Islands off the coast of Washington State, just bigger and with a much greater variety of elements and compounds. But what is the source of this persistent flow of unwanted matter? This question is answered on a weekly basis across America (Figure 7.2). Montanans currently generate a little over eight pounds of solid waste per person per day, which is a little more than the slightly more than seven pounds per American per day[143]. Why is this? Is it because Montana is so remote, meaning Montanans have less affordable access to global recycling networks than do other Americans? Likely. Hawaii's rate of solid waste per day is almost double that of the national average. Is it because of the independent and private nature of most Montanans? Whatever the reason, as Amory Lovins writes in *Reinventing Fire*, in waste streams lie tremendous business and, thus, economic opportunity. What seems to be lacking is a lack of communication, trust, and creativity. There's no reason Montana can't become the entrepreneurial cradle of the West in materials recovery and a leader as a zero-waste state.

FIGURE 7.2. Landfill nutrients reveal themselves on a weekly basis. If successful, this book will help bring our civilization one step closer to eliminating this mode of elimination.

We've all heard or at least suspect that, in nature, there is no waste. No trash cans in The Garden of Eden, remember? Some matter and energy flowing through nature may be considered a burden, some a blessing. Consider water. The rainstorm in New York City resulting from the waste stream of clouds that stalls traffic and ruins hairdos would be more than welcome to the drought-ridden farmers of California. How about sunlight? The waste stream of photons emanating from the sun forces Mississippians to retreat indoors to coal- and gas-powered air-conditioned spaces but brings Californians vacationing at Lake Tahoe out onto their decks for a morning sun-worshipping yoga session.

I'm writing this particular snippet while driving past "Butte, America," home of Evel Knievel and of the world's largest copper mine—"a mile high and a mile deep." Downstream of the Berkeley Pit in Butte and somewhere upstream of Missoula lies an attractive but toxic series of settling ponds designed to prevent heavy metals from reaching the fly-fishing streams that support Montana's tourist sportsman economy. While not considered a landfill per se, this alluring wasteland exists on the outskirts of civilization that eludes most of society. The slow diffusion of elements back into nature in this vast landscape behaves in a manner not unlike the way waste heat from both our bodies and our technologies transpire between the subtle interfaces of energy and matter.

For now, let's just let it settle. For further reading on landfills, please consider the following references: [1, 6, 14, 19, 38, 72, 75, 76, 92, 93, 95, 97, 105, 106, 115, 118, 122, 123, 124, 135, 140, 142]

Organic Waste

Animal waste can be a real issue for watersheds. No one wants to get a big gulp of *E. coli* from a clear mountain stream. One thing to consider weighing, however, is the cost of putting animal waste into the landfill, which has an environmental cost of perhaps one milligram of CO_2 per turd, versus simply letting nature have its way with Bowser's dookie. Animals have been depositing feces in nature since ... well ... since there have been animals.

This is not to say that the best path from an animal's large intestine is straight toward a human's. No, no! The best place for animal waste is in the ground or on the ground away from drinking water, gardening compost, mulched areas where children are playing, places people frolic, or anywhere else where said waste might cause human illness or repulsion.

Despite the title of this book, landfill happens. In fact, the southwest compost pile depicted in 6.1 is a mostly organic landfill. In goes animal waste, cotton, or cellulose-based tampons and other materials and artifacts not suitable for delicate conversation. For a humorous account of one man's battle with the negotiations in feminine products and other regurgitations, I encourage you to read *Regurgitation of a Montana Forester*[131]. At my own household, the issue of how to YIMBY a tampon comes up on a quasi-monthly basis. Since most tampons fall into the category of organic waste, being comprised of cotton and human tissue, they can be readily and safely shared with the fantastic microflora of the non-gardening compost pile (see "Inorganic Waste" in chapter 7).

Banana peels and other fruit peels that may have been sprayed with herbicides and pesticides about which you may be skeptical are also best disposed of in this non-gardening compost pile that is destined for the lawn rather than the garden. Keeping this biomass local is one of the best ways to defy the landfill. If you are worried about the toxicity caused by the fumigation standards to remove insects and other organisms from bananas and other fruits, you may want to consider purchasing organically grown fruits and vegetables. From my own research, most modern pesticides and herbicides lose their molecular structure and, thus, their potency within months or at most, years. This process is accelerated at the higher temperatures reached in an active compost pile.

Inorganic Waste

Inorganic waste consists primarily of elements that you are not likely to find on the back of a cereal box or vitamin bottle. There is no USDA daily recommendation intake amount for cadmium, mercury, lead, or arsenic. Many metals, such as iron, sodium, magnesium, copper, and zinc, do provide essential metabolic functions in our complex bodies. The techno-economic challenge lies in the fact that all these trace elements essential for life are commodities sold at pennies a pound in bulk in the technosphere but at dollars a gram when found in the foodstuffs that we purchase as supplements, thus imitating the biosphere.

The goal in the proper handling of post-consumer inorganic waste is to triage toxic metallic elements and compounds down one stream and put them through various technological catalytic-based refining processes so that they retain their value in the technosphere. Once refined, a few of these metals—such as selenium, copper, magnesium, manganese (check the back of your vitamin bottle for others)—will make their way back into the biosphere ad infinitum. Thinking of it this way, are our bodies now not bridging this technosphere-biosphere gap, inching our way toward that overlap zone seen in Figure 1.8 on page 14?

A lot of our construction waste falls into the inorganic category. Have a look at the contents of the paint cans in your garage. You'll see things like titanium dioxide and other metallic compounds that are at best inert and at worst toxic when ingested. But there they are, in the paint can, serving as building blocks of the technologies that keep us warm and dry, safe and entertained. How best to dispose of these unwanted remnant molecular building blocks of civilization?

As I've already proclaimed, the *build* pathway seems to have the greater value than *bury* or *burn* in general. So to answer the question of what to do with these smaller artifacts of civilization, I've turned toward a sort of bricking of wood pieces for wall building. In Figure 7.2 you can see my slow progress of turning what used to be my neighbor's decking material into a wall for my shed. These little chunks are filling in the gaps between the salvaged slats on the right and the very same pallet that once served as the trailer seen in Figure 5.4 on page 66.

Drywall waste poses another significant challenge. Consider all the little scraps of drywall that emerge from the plumbing and electrician trades—all these circles and squares of paper and gypsum flowing from tradespeople's hands to the floors and dustbins. What if all of this, and I do mean *all of it*, including the mold-remediation waste, were to flow back into the building materials stream? Apply a little heat, and the mold spores return to their elemental form. A little more heat and the water, oxygen, and other volatile molecules gas off. What's left? Well, the same mineral building blocks of gypsum that made the drywall in the first place. Let's take all this mineral waste and rebuild the Last Best Place, your own city, and all points in between!

FIGURE 7.3. Painted lumber being used as part of the *build* solution. The paint on the wood is the remnant of a long-gone neighbor's attempt to either preserve or beautify his deck surface. What will be the fate of what is likely latex (C_xH_y) and a pigment such as titanium dioxide? The fragments of paint as they flake away from my shed will become part of the *bury* stream. When the sun eventually consumes the Earth, or the Rattlesnake Valley ultimately burns, this little speck of matter will become part of the *burn* stream. Regardless of their pending trajectory, up, down or neither, this little layer of paint is in some quantifiable way contributing to the long, steady, and perhaps even accelerating entropization of planet Earth.

Cigarette butts represent a particular conundrum to the 3B model (Figure 7.4). Certainly there are volatile organic compounds trapped in the filter material that could be burned for an additional spurt of energy. Are there organic cigarette filters than can simply be buried? What's the harm in building with them? Why not have a little hole in the living room wall where these little tar traps could be stuffed to slowly accumulate like the old razor blade slots in hotel walls? Might a lifetime's worth of cigarette butt buildup between the living room and the bedroom not offer some acoustic relief to those sleeping as the TV drones on in the room next door? In *Off On Our Own*, Ted Carns shares his own ode to the butt[17].

FIGURE 7.4. Cigarette butts on ground. An unglamorous waypoint in an unglamorous habit.

Dyer lint falls into a similar category with the cigarette butt and the furnace filter (Figure 7.5). With our polyester and nylon clothes, these nearly immortal fibers have no known natural predators other than fire. But do we want to divert these little balls of lint to a fate of flame? How about a little indoor compost pile or bioreactor that breaks down the organic cotton, wool, hemp, pet hair, and silk fibers, leaving the petroleum-derived fibers behind? Let's get this going in elementary school classrooms across the country and around the globe. Send me the data and the photos! Again, referencing Carns, he tells a tale of finding his own hair in a bird's nest on Stone Camp. How apropos that keratin built by Ted Carns's biology was used to build a bird's nest in his own backyard. Another friend of mine puts her dryer lint out for birds to use for nest material. At first glance, this seems innocuous. However, the negative implications of synthetic fibers dispersing themselves indefinitely may outweigh the benefits of providing avian shelters. The jury is out! The experiment has begun! Let the data come back!

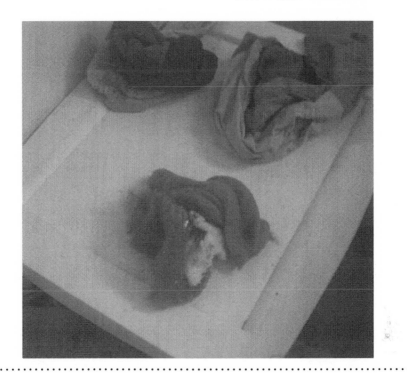

FIGURE 7.5. Dryer lint sitting next to a sock, a washcloth, and a napkin. The lint came from the dryer. The other items came down the laundry chute. This lint is on its way to becoming insulation. Another fate my colleagues and I will pursue is that of phytoremediation.

Dioxins and furans are classes of molecules that you may or may not have heard of. They come in many forms, as do cholesterols, and can be just as confusing and confounding as many of the other midsize molecules that nutritionists and toxicologists build their careers upon and the rest of us wring our hands over. Basically, dioxins and furans are molecules comprised of carbon, oxygen, and chlorine element with molecular weights of approximately 80 to 200. They resemble benzene, a well-known carcinogen found in crude oil. Dioxins and furans have been implicated in human diseases such as cancer and are formed at temperatures of 300° to 800° C in combustion processes[37]. To avoid this toxic fate, higher temperatures must be reached. Higher temperatures and other special treatments of combustion gasses vibrate these midsize molecules apart, shaking them down to simpler, more elemental structures, or simply reduce their probability of formation.[25] From here, these gasses can be filtered or metabolized with relatively simple technologies and biologies.

Waste to Energy

As we move into the future and technologies improve and are refined, alongside emissions regulations becoming more stringent and environmental problems becoming more transparent, we are likely to see more waste-to-energy (WTE) facilities, such as the one recently built in Florida.[26] There is also a firm in Pennsylvania, Sustainable Waste Solutions that has adopted this strategy.[27] Having lived in Palm Beach, Florida, in the early '90s, I can vouch for that region's prolific production of waste. Keep in mind, though, that the 90+ megawatt plant in Florida is still a *thermal facility* that takes the embodied chemical energy of plastics, wood, paper, and other carbon-based materials; combines this energy with oxygen, itself a waste product of photosynthesis; and converts the resulting thermal energy into electricity, waste heat, and carbon dioxide. One of my colleagues has already developed a potential solution to growing wildfires, growing plastic streams, and economic threats to the coal industry (Figure 7.6).

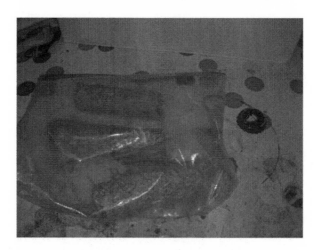

---

[25] http://www.dioxinfacts.org/sources_trends/the_way.html.

[26] http://www.waste360.com/new-projects/story-behind-nation-s-first-new-wte-facility-20-years.

[27] http://www.landfillfree.com/energy-from-waste.html.

Figure 7.6. I have a colleague in Missoula who works with a group that has devised an innovative solution for dealing with the persistent stream of plastics from our homes and businesses and the persistent stream of waste woody biomass from our forestry, timber, and carpentry industries. These MountainPellets, with an energy density greater than Montana coal, have the potential to transform our energy grid.

Another thing to consider as we move forward into the various brave new worlds of biotechnology and energy technology is the rate at which oxygen itself is being depleted from the atmosphere. According to Scripps data, we are losing approximately nineteen out of every one million oxygen molecules from the atmosphere every year[136].[28] Taking a simple linear approach, this implies that we have fifty thousand years of oxygen left, or five thousand years until we've converted 10 percent of the atmosphere's oxygen into carbon dioxide. Clearly, we are in need of either technological or environmental solutions[29] to keep CO_2 levels from rising if we are to steer clear of a runaway greenhouse effect. Time to reinvent fire along with Amory Lovins!

Exercises

1. How far away is your landfill?
2. When was your landfill commissioned?
3. Do a little research and see which countries have the largest landfills. Are there some that don't practice landfilling?
4. Make a list of things that you think belong in a landfill no matter what and post them online on Twitter @BradLayton, @ZWLBP, or #ZWLBP.

---

[28] http://scrippso2.ucsd.edu/.

[29] http://breakingenergy.com/2015/06/03/why-we-need-to-get-from-carbon-capture-storage-ccs-to-carbon-capture-utilization-ccu/.

8

Integrated Solutions

This chapter introduces combustion-free thermal, biochemical, and human-powered strategies for dealing with waste. The primary goal of each of these technologies is to preserve our technological advancement and prowess with this triple bottom-line set of goals in mind:

1. Enhance quality of human life
2. Preserve our fossil fuel reserves for future generations
3. Allow other animals on the planet, which sustain our own lives, to flourish

Hey, perhaps this could be the new mantra for the Environmental Protection Agency!

Solar Forge

In summer 2013, several talented students of the University of Montana's Energy Technology Program built a simple, bare-bones device capable of melting old candles into a large tribute to that year's summer practicum. This relatively low-tech device was built from little more than a Fresnel lens, as is commonly found in large projection television screens, a wooden frame, and some firebricks.

FIGURE 8.1. The solar forge in action at the 2013 Summer Energy Technology Practicum. Note the bright spot in the middle of the firebricks, which themselves appear shaded. Also note the use of welding goggles necessary to view this white-hot nucleus of fire-free heat.

Upon seeing pennies liquefy within three to four seconds of being exposed to a concentrated blast of solar radiation, we very quickly made the distinction between temperature and heat. The Fresnel funnels all the photons that would have otherwise distributed their heat evenly over the ground into a single focal point in the forge, thus rapidly raising the temperature of a small volume of space. If an unfortunate fragment of matter happens to find itself in this small volume, a nearly instantaneous phase change takes place. With this forge, we were able to melt down several used candles into a homogenized single candle with five nice wicks for a flowerlike effect.

The forge was also used to melt precious metals reclaimed from discarded computers. Typically this thermal process is accomplished with a propane torch. The solar forge, however, was able to accomplish the solid to liquid phase change with no combustion, essentially reinventing fire.

Phytoremediation, Fermentation, Gasification, Pyrolysis, and Torrefaction (vs. Incineration)

Before diving into this little catchall section, I want to briefly dive down a rabbit hole that frequently opens in my academic office. This channel of prolific pondering that persistently presents itself is none other than perpetual motion. As far as we humans have observed, the universe itself and its constituents *are* in constant motion, at least at the molecular scale. This is a consequence of the third law of thermodynamics, which states that a temperature of absolute zero cannot be either maintained or even attained, however briefly. Does a similar principle hold true for our global civilization?

Our civilization will always require an energy source that we will continuously degrade into heat to perpetuate our civilization until it reaches its fate.[30] For example, it is rumored that Sweden has become so effective at recycling that it no longer has a sufficient supply of waste to power its waste-to-energy technologies and must therefore import garbage for energy.

This constant motion observation and our persistent need for energy leads us to the conclusion that humans must always keep their internal and external fires burning to survive and thrive. For our warm-blooded corporeal selves living as far as we do from thermodynamic equilibrium, we are persistently answering the perplexing question: What is Life?[114] What Schrödinger tells us is that life is literally an internal fire.

The external technological fires that power civilization must continue to burn as well. How else to move our trains, fly our planes, spin our turbines, cook our food, clean our homes, and maintain all the other vital functions of civilization? The point here is that just as matter is never truly at rest, neither shall we as individuals or as a global civilization be at rest so long as we shall live.

All this harnessing of primary energy that we perform is for the general purpose of deentropicizing our bodies and our surroundings or, in other words, making our bodies and our surroundings cleaner, safer, and more predictable. With this in mind, let's examine each of the six physical processes mentioned in the title of this section to see how each of them fits into the bigger picture of sustainability, waste management, and, yes, perpetual motion.

---

[30] https://www.youtube.com/watch?v=GOrWy_yNBvY.

Think of the six processes in the chapter title as rings of Heaven or if you prefer rings of Hades. Each one involves a greater energy level and conversion of matter from complex components into simpler components.

The first process, *phytoremediation*, is essentially the cleanup or concentration of microscale and nanoscale technological contaminants via biological means. Phytomass is the general term for carbon-based, living matter that recently received energy from the sun. Phytoremediation can either concentrate toxins within a plant or culture of single-celled organisms or exclude them, essentially performing the same sorting tasks that the recycling technologist performs, but at the molecular level. Phytoremediation occurs at ambient temperatures and pressures, in the presence or absence of oxygen, and typically takes a long time—days to years. A common example of this is the use of switchgrass to pull heavy metals from soils.

The second process, *fermentation*, also involves the breakdown of larger complex molecules such as sugars into smaller, simpler molecules such as ethanol. The energy stored in the molecular bonds of sugars drives these biochemical reactions. Think of this like the little snap, crackle, pop that you hear when eating cereal. Each one of those little bursts of energy power the reactions that keep your cells powered. Ethanol, of course, is a mild toxin that we consume to diminish stress and inhibitions, enhance creativity, and numb a variety of pains. Other simple alcohols serve as sterilizers and even fuels, thus perpetuating the usefulness of these small, carbon-based molecules.

Gasification is the process by which solid matter that contains water and other volatile organic compounds is heated to a high temperature (>700°C) that produces gas. If this gas is steam or water vapor, it has many obvious immediate uses. If the gas is carbon monoxide, hydrogen, methane, or other simple hydrocarbons, it can be used for combustion to produce heat for hot water, maintain indoor temperatures, or even make electricity.

Pyrolysis occurs at temperatures of 300 to 600° C and typically creates purer streams of gas and solids. The gasses coming off are typically carbonaceous and can thus be burned with oxygen. This heat can then be used to drive a turbine to make electricity and either used locally or sold to your local utility through a power purchase agreement.

Torrefaction, a mild pyrolysis, occurs at a lower temperature (200 to 300° C) than gasification and may be employed to create carbon-rich solid fuels, hydrocarbon distillates, and/or gaseous by-products.

Each of these five processes is an alternative to the sixth—*incineration*, which is simply mindless combustion. Think of the five alternative processes like chewing, digesting, or controlled internal combustion, as opposed to the senseless acts of suicide bombing or car bombing. The five gentle, controlled processes are creative construction, rather than mindless destruction.

For a much deeper dive into the worlds of perpetual motion, read the works of Prigogine, who illuminates the fascinating world of subdynamics within the context of fossil fuel extraction[104].

Hazmats

This little section of the book will not begin to do justice to the vast and growing world of hazmat (hazardous materials) handling, disposal, and repurposing. But suffice it to say that hazmats are any materials that have obvious harmful side effects to humans and to the natural environment, if given the opportunity to interact with human flesh or to simply diffuse into the environment. In lieu of providing technical guidance on where, when, why, and how hazardous materials are processed, I submit here a sample of one of my student's work from NRGY 270 Recycling Technology, Fall Semester, 2015. Sean Doty writes:

> I worked on several projects and volunteered at two events throughout the semester to experience the fates of municipal waste. My first experience was at Hazardous Waste Days in Missoula. This event was put on by the Missoula Valley Water Quality District. The purpose of this event was to keep hazardous waste out of Missoula's aquifer and send it somewhere to be used as a fuel or disposed of in a safe manner. There was no charge to residents to dispose of hazardous materials and over 1,100 vehicles passed through the event. All told, there were sixteen volunteers working in shifts during the two days. These volunteers included students from the University of Montana, several

Missoula City firefighters, a professional chemist, and citizens from the community. The types of materials collected were comprised of petroleum products, paints, aerosol cans, mercury-containing products, fluorescent tubes, herbicides, pesticides, as well as acids and bases.

The total material collected at the event is summarized in the table.

Table 8.1 Type and amount of material collected at Missoula Valley Water District's Hazardous Waste Days on September 19, 2015.

Quantity	Material
3,900 lbs	special wastes: pesticides, solvents, acids, & bases
55 gal	lead paint
1,760 gal	liquid paint
608 gal	paint sludge
700 gal	spent antifreeze
810 gal	spent motor oil
3.5 cubic yards	aerosol paint cans
3,600 linear feet	fluorescent tubes
three 5-gal buckets	mercury products
two 55 gal drums	special waste aerosols

A little arithmetic reveals that this particular Hazardous Waste Days in the Last Best Place, each vehicle dropped off an average of about thirty pounds of waste material. With an average vehicle weight of over three thousand pounds and over one-third of the total mass, the efficiency of this process isn't great. But what's the alternative? The single largest mass was in liquid paint, most or all of which could have gone to Home Resource.

Perhaps this little peek into a single day in the life of hazmats in Missoula stresses the need to avoid the buildup of these fluids in the first place. Just as you return your bottles and bags to the grocery store, take your unused toxic fluids to a place in your community, like Missoula's own Home Resource, which will give you a tax break for donating used materials and sell them to your neighbor for a small fee so they can stay in business. Do this during your next trip to purchase more goods for the next round of reshaping civilization.

Exercises

1. What repurposing do you already do? Have you ever used a phone book to sit on? Have you used old materials for decoration?
2. How do matter and energy interact at your home? Do you have a fireplace? Do you have a sink disposal?
3. What would it take to become net positive?

9

War Stories

Summer Intern – I recently had the privilege of having an intern for the summer. He was a self-proclaimed "third-generation garbage man" with a passion for the American Dream, economic sustainability, and giving back to his nation and community. Since I didn't have any financial capital of my own to invest in this young man, I had to get creative with ways to compensate him while we organized materials and artifacts around my house, which also serves as the address for my business, Human Powered Future PLLC. For example, I gave him all the spare change that came through the slot in the dining room wall. I split a ten-dollar bill with him that my neighbor paid us to remove some old railroad tie landscaping from her yard. This is a story in itself, which led to a discussion at our homeowner association and some spirited interactions with my NIMBY neighbors who did not want railroad timbers in the common areas between our houses. In lieu of a salary, I fed him lunch. I made him laugh and I put him in touch with a few other recycling firms in town.

Whether or not these little adventures in the Land of YIMBY with my intern will pay off for him financially as he launches his own company, ReIndustries, remains to be seen, but what does seem clear from this type of mentorship and apprenticeship interaction is that we are indeed reaching a tipping point or phase shift in our economy. Specifically, we are moving away from a linear economy of conquer, claim, corral, commoditize, capitalize, and crash for the sake of short-term profits for the few to a circular economy of rejuvenate, revive, recycle, rejoin, and repeat[44].

Zero Waste in a Small Space – The morning I was writing this section, I was preparing lunch for my mother, who was arriving from Traverse City, Michigan, in Grand Rapids, Michigan. As I was putting food on the table in a small rented kitchen, I mistook some rotting chicken for some well-aged cheese. Whoa! The error was soon detected by my daughter, and the chicken had to be wasted. Unpleasant and true. Since I have been sticking to my zero-landfill rule and did not have immediate access to a compost pile in the small house my family and I were in, I was faced with a burn or bury fate for the chicken. The chicken, of course, was purchased to build human tissue. Fearing that it might cause unpleasant odors in the fireplace and knowing that I would not likely soon establish a critical mass of compost, I elected the bury option and chucked the chicken down the sink disposal. This of course led to a waste of water as my daughter and I washed the foul chicken smell from our hands. Once in the sewer, decomposition gasses from the chicken tissue could be used for heat in a place such as the Gaslight District of East Grand Rapids.

The Coffee Cup – Another case in point to define waste is the single-use cup next to me that I just used to drink coffee from on the airplane I'm riding in. I'm still debating whether or not to take it with me for my next two flights back to Missoula, rather than placing it in the "garbage" that the flight attendant is calling for.

The "disposable" cup next to me on that flight back to the Last Best Place certainly has, or had, a few more lives to live as a cup, allowing it to stay in the "build" realm. It could also be used to start a garden in the spring, facilitating the bury mode, or it could be burned for its thermal value. In nearly every case, from a sustainability standpoint, the "build" mode is the most preferable.

In its broadest definition, waste can be viewed simply as inefficiency. In the case of wasted food, there is financial and material inefficiency: Money and energy must be spent to purchase animal flesh or vegetable tissue that was not used as human fuel, and subsequent energy must be purchased to pump purified water into a household to deal with the oversight in a sanitary manner. If we refused to use disposable coffee cups, airlines and coffee shops could be spared the expense of bringing on unnecessary matter, purchasing the cups in the first place, and paying for their disposal. This begs the deeper philosophical discussion of whether waste is somehow inherent to maintaining a robust economy.

I'm sure that many readers and certainly most Americans might scoff at the idea of obsessing over the fate of one little coffee cup. It's just one silly, little cup! But what if no more coffee cups were supplied by airlines? The result would be thousands of tons of natural resources per year staying put in the biosphere (with the elimination of paper cups) or remaining as petrochemical resources for future generations (with that of plastic cups).

The Couch – During the summer of 2015, when my neighbor was loading up his dump trailer to make a run to the landfill, I challenged myself to zee-dub its contents. I pulled out the branches and weeds for my compost pile; collected the aluminum cans for my other neighbor, who uses the income from recycling them to pay for her son's dental work; and packaged up the conventional plastics, metals, and glass for recycling. The major challenge was the circa 1985 couch that had been sitting outside in the elements for several years. I went at the fabric and padding with a claw hammer and pliers, took out the springs, and recovered all the fasteners. Some of the wood became kindling, but one of the stouter boards became curtain rod brackets for my living room. The biggest challenge, though, was the fabric, which I ended up stuffing in my laundry room sink. As I did a load of laundry, the old fabric became cleaner in the gray water from the wash. It didn't make sense to me to waste energy-intensive potable water on this old fabric. I then hung it out to dry and took it to Goodwill. Just like magic, the couch disappeared!

The Above-Ground Pool – If you haven't heard of Craigslist by now, perhaps you haven't been online much lately. It's not only a great place to find like-minded individuals but also a great place to turn trash into treasure. Recently, a friend of mine in town, Shannon Cleg, was on the verge of being compelled to landfill a swimming pool as he readied his backyard for a graduation party. I called my neighbor and partner in crime, Nenelait—pronounced "nay-nay-lay"—to see if she might want it for her backyard. Being the closet packrat and opportunist that she is, she instantly said, "Yes."

I popped as much of Shannon's pool into my car as I could, leaving the rest for her to grab in her rig. Upon getting the whole assembly home, however, both of our spouses protested. Our better, saner, and less impulsive halves won the day, and Nenelait and I decided the pool had to go. But where? I listed it for fifty dollars on Craigslist with a photo of what it looks like new and, within three hours, was in a three-way texting bidding war on my phone and sold it for seventy-five. This was enough money to sponsor a small block party, where neighbors had a chance to catch up, and Nenelait and I got to plan our next conspiracy.

Talking Trash!

One hope of mine is that we can replace the words *garbage* and *trash* with the word *landfill*. Try it. Instead of saying *garbage* or *trash* just say *landfill*. Once we look forward to the next destination of the matter in our hands, do we really want to leave a legacy of adding to Mount Methane in the Last Best Place, or any place for that matter? Take this one step further and ask if we want to leave this legacy for the *only* place?"[31]

A Little Thinking Out Loud

At this point in the book, you have read a fairly accurate account of how I have been able to take my own home to the point of zero waste, and indeed to a landfill-negative status. Any typical material or artifact you would like to name, I will gladly accept the challenge of providing a nonpolluting, nonlandfilling path into the future. To do so, please contact me at layton.bradley@gmail.com. I will gladly post the solutions on my YouTube channel[32] or Twitter account @BradLayton. What follows in this section are a few additional thoughts that tie in the practical advice with a few academic and philosophical ruminations.

Entropy, Information, and Economics – In addition to feeding my obsession with zero waste, I have also been feeding an obsession of

---

[31] Well, it's the only place until Elon Musk and his team at SpaceX succeed in their Mars spaceships, which, if his recent biography is accurate, will be powered with methane[139]. So maybe we do want to build that Empire State Building's worth of garbage every year and launch from Mount Methane. Let's start using our Tetra Paks and Bota Box wine bags to capture the methane rather than "destroying" it through combustion as we currently do. On to Mars with our garbage-powered rockets!

[32] https://www.youtube.com/user/BradleyLayton.

attempting to understand what formal relationship might exist among thermodynamic entropy, binary information, and economic wealth. To this end, I have written a pair of papers that attempt to establish a framework for further discussion and research[71,72]. These academic works are essentially my own version of the triple-bottom-line problem, where we are all attempting to become wealthier; maintain an intelligent, informed, happy brain; and avoid further environmental degradation. While the connection to this line of reasoning and zero waste may seem tenuous at first, there are many connections, most of which dovetail with the naysayers and YIMBY references listed earlier.

For example, while I may be avoiding the financial cost of $300 per year to pay for a curbside landfill service, this adds disorder and entropy to my home in the form of many random bits of matter cluttering my garage. On the flipside, it is my hope that, by assembling the information in the book in the way that I have, this may lead to financial gain through royalties resulting from book sales. What remains to be seen, however, and a question I hope to follow up on in a more formal manner, is whether or not my burn habits in the fireplace of 8 Columbine Road do in fact offset the fracked natural gas that is piped to my house in a real, measureable way that diminishes the rate at which we diminish nonrenewable carbon resources[113]. If you, the reader, have any interest in pursuing sustainability on a global scale, Schramski, Gattie, and Brown's 2015 paper is one of the most important and compelling I have read on the topic. Several of my YouTube videos discuss it at length.

Plastic Beaches and Plastic Crowns – As I write this little section of this little book, I'm listening to Stiv Wilson's April 26, 2016, talk at the University of Montana in Missoula. He's talking about his journey around the world and witnessing the plastic beaches in the Philippines. He's also speaking of his many successes in moving legislation forward to keep plastics out of the biosphere. Since I tend to carry my laptop nearly everywhere I go, and I love on-the-spot inspiration, I couldn't help but pop in a visual example from my own experience in gleaning plastics from the biosphere. The colorful medley of human detritus was collected while throwing a few sticks and logs for my dog on a Lake Michigan public beach over Easter weekend 2016 (Figure 9.1). Seeing this little pile on the driveway in East Grand Rapids after returning from our little jaunt makes me think of the four-dimensional path that all matter takes through space-time. What would it take to map all these fragments of our modern life back to their sources? What a tangled web we weave!

FIGURE 9.1. These plastics were all collected in a twenty-minute period over a hundred-yard stretch of beach on the shores of Lake Michigan over Easter weekend 2016. These were the big, obvious pieces. How many pieces are already buried in the sand? How many tiny pieces are floating out upon the waters being ingested by wildlife? It's a bit of a *Where's Waldo?* isn't it? See if you can find the letter *H*, a tampon, a lip balm container, a hair barrette, shotgun shell wads, a balloon string, and a few cigar holders.

Before getting too worked up over the amount of plastic bobbing around in the world's waters, don't think that it's just a water thing. Here are some discarded artifacts a friend and I found at the crown of the continent. Yes, these little plastic egg and the fragments of this plastic spoon were found on the North American Continental Divide, midway between Bozeman and Missoula (Figure 9.2). Public apologies to the wee people who may have been counting on these durable structures for housing!

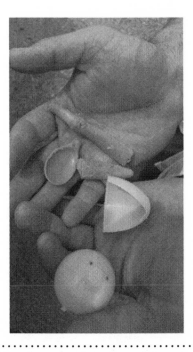

FIGURE 9.2. These plastic fragments from discarded artifacts were gleaned from a public access trail on the Continental Divide between Missoula and Bozeman. In the image shown in Figure 9.1, the question was what the path from human hand to lakeshore must have looked like. In this case, the question becomes what would the path from human hand to ocean or lakeshore look like had other human hands not interceded?

Leadership and Transformation – On my own forefront of affecting public policy, I have been striving to enact a zero-waste protocol at the University of Montana that would take the institution off the landfill. One of the more challenging waste streams consists of thin film plastics—shopping bags, candy wrappers, snack packaging, and the like. All these pesky little flakes of processed petroleum are currently headed for a fate of bury. But is landfilling really the best use for plastic in the Last Best Place? How about a residence built with plastic bales? Why not distill it using the Japanese company Blest's solid-to-liquid distillation technology that came up during my talk in Japan? How about investing in the MountainPellet? Once we realize as a species that our survival and happiness depends on sharing and cooperation rather than distrust and competition, we will truly enter an age of enlightenment.

111

Certainly humans will continue to innovate, and our technologies will evolve. Perhaps someday we will move away from plastic packaging. For the time being, until we turn off this petro tap and move toward bioplastics, in the interest of maximum utility, a waste-to-energy approach to thin film plastic waste appears to be optimal. At least one technical solution already exists—collection, baling, shredding, and extrusion into a composite pellet that is currently being used at the Flambeau River Papers in Wisconsin. This pellet is then burned in an EPA-approved cofiring plant. And as I write this, my colleagues and I are working on a suite of technologies to capture the greenhouse gasses, collect them, and turn them into carbon-rich soil amendments, thus returning carbon to the soil in a solid, nourishing form, rather than skyward in a polluting form. In addition to the logistical issues, some of the challenges are political. However, if the University of Montana's president were to immediately declare that the University of Montana were going to go off the landfill, he would be an immediate hero, and students from across the country and around the world would return to this Shangri-la of a town in droves.

As part of my tenure package, I was required to submit examples of how I have excelled at teaching, research, and service. At Missoula College, the majority of this decision is based upon the teaching record. As part of my personal strategy, and in order to maximize the efficacy of my time, I have engaged in and led activities that embody elements of all three metrics. For example, I held a zero-waste activity during the 2015 Missoula Made Fair (Figures 9.3 and 9.4).

FIGURE 9.3. At the 2016 Made Fair in Missoula, which strives to keep dollars local through the purchasing of crafts from local artisans, my Recycling Technology students, along with the Zero Waste Bucket group of the Climate Smart Initiative in Missoula, decided to zero-waste the event by diverting all landfill-bound materials to more noble destinations. In the figure above, you see ground zero of this effort, where we separated materials and artifacts based upon the principles described in this book. What a blast!

One of the more remarkable discoveries of our zero-waste efforts at the 2015 Made Fair was the relatively small volume of waste once everything had been sorted and triaged.

FIGURE 9.4. Sorted cups from the 2015 Made Fair. Once sorted by material type, the volume of waste generated was about 10 percent of what it would have been had it been left in garbage bags on its way to the landfill. What if the people who purchased these three hundred or so beverages had brought their own cups? We can get there more easily than we might expect.

Carbon accounting – Assuming that we could collect the ton or so of plastic that flows out of the University of Montana every day and bale it for energy production, we would then need to either ship it to a manufacturing or waste-to-energy facility or build such a facility locally, which also exacts an energy and economic tax. Assuming we then convert this plastic to energy or durable goods by reacting it with oxygen in the atmosphere or an annealing heat source, we then have the issue of dealing with the resulting carbon dioxide from energy consumption.

Some of the best solutions that I've seen for taking CO_2 from a gaseous phase to a solid phase involve biochemical pathways. For example, algae and many other microorganisms have enzymes that have been evolving since life began to strip the carbon atom from the oxygen atoms, thus allowing the carbon to serve as a building block of life and the oxygen to be released as a waste product into the atmosphere. This movement of gaseous carbon dioxide from the atmosphere into the biosphere typically requires a flow of photons from the sun to drive this process. There may also be organisms that can perform a similar biologically driven sequestration that requires a chemothermal gradient rather than an electromagnetic one. Investigation for a naturally occurring organism with this trait, or even the genetic engineering of this type of biochemical pathway, is highly warranted as we attempt to suck the waste gasses of our industrial economy out of the atmosphere.

Embrace Reality – By now you have most likely noted that, for the average American making $20,000 per year ($10 an hour), spending up to an hour per day ($300 a year) dealing with creative ways to avoid the landfill to save money is likely to cost more in time than it does in money. So let's be clear: Money is a human artifact, not a naturally occurring entity. Money exists solely as a faith-based system, not unlike religion. Whereas most religions have a faith in a life beyond the earthly life, money is merely a faith in the future[58]. Specifically, money is, at its core, a faith that there will be more money in the future than there is now. This is the central tenet of capitalism and may explain why we tend to see more consistent traffic at banks than we do churches, mosques, and temples.

Try this for a visualization of money: Start with a single point having one positive and one negative arrow coming out of it between two individuals. In an ideal world, the arrows have the same length—one person's loss is exactly the other's gain, and all is equal in space and time. However, as we know, the person with more money will likely value each dollar less than that of the person with less money, leading to a trade imbalance[91]. The opposite is also possible, where the person with more money will value each individual dollar more than the person with less money, leading to a lopsided distribution of wealth that we see in today's economy. Either way, the system is dynamic, and, as we have seen with our multiple recessions and the Great Depression, the system can become unstable, and this agreed-upon, intangible artifact can creep into the real world with terrible lasting repercussions.

If we now take the step and equate money with commodities that ultimately must be dealt with as waste, we must ask the question of whether or not waste is inherent in maintaining a robust economy. Is every step along the way of our techno-economic metabolism at both the large and small scales simply a tiny loop in a waste stream, or perhaps just a little waste eddy?

It is now up to us to decide to deal with all the waste that we generate, rather than leaving the burden of dealing with landfills to future generations. As we've seen up to this point in this book, solutions and opportunities abound.

Dumpster Diving in the Infinite Corridor – Now for a few final thoughts on food waste in this chapter on war stories. I have lived a little bit of this scavenging for food lifestyle myself. While in college, I used to dive down a particular garbage chute when the doughnut cart would close in Lobby 7 at MIT. The cart would close at around one in the afternoon, and the unpurchased food would be tossed into a gently sloping chute. The vendor never seemed to chuck the bag all the way in to the point that it would drop off into the vertical abyss beyond. I would dive into this door, sometimes to the point that just my toes held me from sliding farther in. I would grab the bag, pick out the two or three remaining morsels and head up to physics recitation. I was a broke, hungry, high-metabolism rower, with only a few hours until the next blistering practice on the muddy Charles River. That free fat, sugar, and starch came in handy.

When reflecting on this period of my life and the movement toward zero food waste, an immediate dilemma emerges: What if everybody behaved this way? If everybody behaved this way, there would be lines by the dumpster at Outback Steakhouse instead of lines at the front door. There would be reduced incentive to sell food for money. However, if there were financial mechanisms put in place whereby a grocery store or restaurant were able to claim food waste that went to feed people, rather than a compost pile or a landfill, as a tax-deductible business loss, it could be a win for everyone. Grocery stores and restaurants would eliminate their need for a landfill subscription, they would save money on taxes, their patrons would still get fed, low-income individuals would likely eat better than they otherwise would, and stores and restaurants that adopted this zero-waste model would likely gain enhanced revenue by adopting sustainability practices. And humanity's demands on the natural environment would diminish.

Strings Too Short to Use – In addition to this book serving as a how-to guide, it has also served as a self-help text for me. When I moved to Missoula in 2010, I expected a clean, pristine utopia devoid of litter, devoid of crime, devoid of injustice, devoid of poverty. But the same ills that plague the rest of civilization are here as well. Perhaps not to the extremes as other cities experience, but there are cans and bottles on the street; people shoot each other on occasion; and shady, nepotistic practices abound unfortunately. Some of this is based on true shortage. Most of it, in my opinion, is based on either ignorance or fear, not true shortage or scarcity of life-sustaining goods and services. Just as with any book written with honesty and passion, *Zero Waste in the Last Best Place* has been a journey for me into how my early habits and those of my ancestors brought me to this point in my life. So here in "A Little Thinking Out Loud," I can't help but think that a lot of our habits carry over from either real memories of want in our lives or historical events like the Great Depression that our recent relatives have lived through. One such insight comes to mind—a story I hadn't thought about in quite some time. My mother used to tell me about the time she and her mother were cleaning out the attic of one of her aunts after she passed away. One of the more peculiar discoveries was a glass jar labeled "string too short to use."

The End Game

Ode to a Cigarette Butt – In *Off On Our Own,* Ted Carns goes into what I call *Ode to a Cigarette Butt.* He speaks of how he noticed a small, white feature on a rock face somewhere that he thought might be a fleck of snow, or maybe a mushroom, or perhaps some sort of mineral deposit, or maybe a bird dropping. He saw it intermittently and continued to wonder what it was until finally he had the opportunity to scale the necessary distance to investigate the tiny speck's identity. When he finally had it in his hands, he realized that it was a cigarette butt that had gotten itself lodged in a small crevice and that it was more or less doing its job obeying the first law of thermodynamics, just persisting, not decaying, conserving its material state. Indefinitely.

Ted's conclusion of his little obsessive ode was that, in the world of recycling, time becomes irrelevant. Everything will eventually be recycled and recycled ad infinitum. Just look at the mountains themselves, grains of sand on the beach, and all the leaves on all trees. Under the conditions we experience on Earth, matter does not simply decay—at least not at an appreciable rate. Of course E does equal mc squared. Matter and energy will continue their intertwined dance for time immemorial, but Ted's point in pondering the cigarette butt is that, if he did not take the initiative to recycle or repurpose this discarded artifact, nature herself would eventually find a way.

117

Of course, this cigarette butt would eventually lose it structure. The fibers it consisted of would eventually depolymerize in the sun's rays and then eventually reenter the biosphere through its elemental constituents. But wasn't this butt a little out of place in nature? Maybe, maybe not. Perhaps it would become the makings of a bird's nest, reaching the fate of the lint that my friend in Bozeman gives back to nature. Anyway, Ted picked up the cigarette butt, brought it home, and placed it in his cigarette butt bucket, along with the other ones that friends, acquaintances, passersby, or other unknown people had left along the way. One might wonder, will this bucket ever fill? What use could one possibly have for a big pile of cigarette butts? Why keep them in a bucket at all? Just burn them, Ted. Just bury them, Ted. Just build with them, Ted. Maybe by now he has. Maybe by now he's found a commercial use for them, like repurposing them as filters for a chimney, or stuffing them into a wall cavity for insulation, or using them as a substrate for growing exotic mushrooms. Maybe I'll get a chance to ask him someday.

Our Swirling NASCAR Reality – On a deeper philosophical level, very little of the matter that's here on planet Earth right now is going anywhere in the near future. The last time that happened, the moon was formed. So our civilization, which is based on the exchange of money, ideas, and matter, is a little like a NASCAR race: Everything is cyclically swirling with varying degrees of control and precision. Leaders emerge and are replaced. Crashes punctuate the persistent motion as the lead changes, but the looming question is what the future will hold. Every NASCAR fan has his or her favorite driver, each investor has his or her favorite stock, each philosopher has his or her favorite idea, but nothing really enters or leaves; only the configuration of matter changes.

Taking a philosophical approach and conceding that, at any given time, all matter is in a temporary state, on its way to becoming another compound or artifact, will we not conclude that, eventually, 100 percent of all materials will eventually go to waste? We have this conversation as part of our Zero Waste Bucket meetings within the Climate Smart Initiative team in Missoula frequently. And indeed, it seems to be true. Everything you see around you is ephemeral. Your own body, and indeed all organic and technological systems, are merely positioned within some material stream or another and gleaning a portion of nearby matter and energy to sustain their metabolisms or to build their reserves[30].

With the recent establishment of the International Big History Association and other works by prominent scientists such as Steven Hawking, we appear to have a reasonable handle on where we came from and how we arrived in our current state. There are other authors, such as Ray Kurzweil, who have painted a picture of what the future may hold for us. Authors Neil deGrasse Tyson and Martin Rees have looked into the deep future for a look at how the entire planet may be recycled by the cosmos. For now, though, we must become more responsible in our role of tending to The Garden.

If you follow the Gaia hypothesis, you are aware that Earth itself is basking in the *waste radiation* of the sun, earthworms are eating their way through *waste leaves, seeds, bug carcasses, and other organic detritus*, and processing this tree manna into soil. Trees and plants are breathing the *waste carbon dioxide* exhaled by animals. Evaporated water generated from *waste heat* falls back to Earth as water or snow and erodes solid rock to create the *waste sands and soils* that literally support life. So just as Schrödinger's cat is simultaneously alive and dead, all matter is simultaneously waste and not. A similar theme of dual realities was visited in the movie *Back to the Future*. In one version Marty's nemesis Biff becomes president. Crime and corruption ensue. But in reality, Marty prevails and peace and prosperity abound. To realize a clean, and prosperous future, we must start with this perspective, build the capacity and maintain the desire. If we all envision a clean, green, fertile planet, this reality will manifest itself.

At some point, a formal history of waste study is warranted. This might best start with the small crumb of rock we find ourselves upon, move through the fossil record, head on into archaeology and then to the middens, and progress through the Industrial Revolution and into our current era. My suspicion is that we are simultaneously accumulating waste at the macroscale and the atomic scale at a rate that will force major adaptation and innovation. We must look to global solutions to swirl upward to a progressive, enlightened state, rather than downward into a cynical and destructive state.

A Little Peek into Human Power

By now you've detected my sustainability obsession. On a personal level, this frequently entails a dedication to using my own energy, rather than that stored in the bowels of the Earth, to move waste and biomass. Living in a relatively compact community like Missoula and relying almost exclusively on my bicycles for transportation, I had the compulsion one day to rescue a log from the river's edge for the purpose of landscaping and soil building at my home. This expedition resulted in the much anticipated and unlikely photo seen in Figure 9.5.

FIGURE 9.5. A two-inch ball hitch on the Surly Big Dummy was used to tow some driftwood home. This substantial chunk of cellulose is becoming soil at 8 Columbine as you read this.

Exercises

1. What is your philosophy of waste? Jot down a few ideas. Come back to this later and write a little more.
2. Have you ever hesitated to throw something away? What did you do with it instead? Where is it now?
3. What are some of your first memories of garbage or trash? Is it satisfying or slightly disturbing?

10

National Recycling Companies

I recently came across a story of a young man who had dropped out of Princeton to make worm castings for a friend who was growing marijuana. His epiphany about turning food waste into money to keep people wasted led to the founding of TerraCycle. You can now find the company's logo on many single-use packages (Figure 10.1). This is just one of many companies that have come up with solutions for upcycling difficult-to-recycle artifacts, such as the ubiquitous juice box.

FIGURE 10.1. The TerraCycle logo on a single-use food container.

Markets for Materials

There is a market for absolutely everything. Troll around <u>recycling</u>.net, <u>polycycle</u>.net, <u>waste</u>.net, and other websites devoted to repurposing. In his research for starting his company, ReIndustries, my friend, former intern, and now colleague Nathan Hansen found an unexpected market in baled, high-density polyethylene (think grocery bag or milk jug). It sells for approximately five hundred dollars per ton, whereas ancient, nonrenewable coal is being sold for eight dollars per ton from the Treasure State. How can it be that we are essentially giving away this precious, nonrenewable resource and then turning around and paying Republic to build Mount Methane with a commodity that is selling for more than sixty times the price? Yet again, Amory Lovins wins the day by exposing our economic insanity.

The big markets are global, and as my NRGY 270 Recycling Technology students discovered in the fall of 2015, the big markets have monthly requirements in the hundreds or even thousands of tons. Clearly, this is not a class project to be completed in a single semester. However, if the Last Best Place is to tap into these global markets, we need to begin taking Missoula Mayor John Engen's Proclamation Moving Missoula Toward Zero Waste Month seriously, reread the Quick-Start, 12-Step Guide in chapter 1, and refuse to make refuse. Let's get Montana Rail Link on board for this bold venture; mine Mount Methane just as PCS Biofuels has begun to do in Vancouver, British Columbia; and capitalize both financially and physically on the assets we pay to have removed from our homes, workplaces, and places of worship.

Perhaps one of the most exciting and promising markets is the emerging carbon market. Keegan Eisenstadt of ClearSky Climate Solutions in Missoula has extensive experience negotiating international carbon trades whereby a polluter in Europe will pay an indigenous population intending to financially profit from agricultural practices to *not* cut down their forests[82]. In Eisenstadt's brokering model, a penalty cost has been placed on the emission of carbon dioxide from a technology that bursts carbon bonds with photosynthetically manufactured oxygen and sends them skyward as carbon dioxide. This penalty cost is then injected into the economy of a community rich in trees and land but poor in dollars. This progressive model allows the biosphere to remain intact and the technosphere to persist, while slowing the acceleration in sea rise we expect to see as a result of the accumulation of greenhouse gasses in the atmosphere. To put this into our 3B model, the carbon dioxide *burned* to power our industrial practices enters the atmosphere, and big healthy trees *build* themselves. These trees may then be used to *build* houses or may end up *buried* for soil *building* and further propagation of the forest, resulting in carbon sequestration ad infinitum or ad Ω[113].

What remains to be seen in the carbon markets is whether or not anticipated coastal real estate losses, as well as soil salinization, will be factored into the costs of emitting carbon. On my visit to Japan, I was able to witness the building of a twenty-nine-meter seawall at the Onagawa Nuclear Power Plant near Sendai. The previous wall was fourteen meters tall and just barely held back the 2011 tsunami that took out Fukushima. This new looming monolith foreshadows what lies ahead as more waste carbon dioxide accumulates in the atmosphere. It's time to find integrated solutions.

The Atlanta Airport, which generates approximately seventy tons of waste per day, has addressed the issue with a slogan "You Trash. We Sort. It's Recycled." A company, Waste Pro USA, transports waste using nonconventionally fueled trucks to a material recovery facility (MRF), where it is presumably sorted by hand. A recent article in the Hartsfield-Jackson News reported that "All recyclable materials are recycled and the rest is sent to landfills." For more on this see the sustainability page on the airport's website[33] reports that "All recyclable materials are recycled, and the rest is sent to landfills." My question is what's "the rest?" It would be a shame to have food waste from the airport heading to landfills, especially in light of the Pope's recent article[46].

In his landmark work on economic theory, *The Origin of Wealth*, Eric D. Beinhocker describes a place in Manila known as Smokey Mountain (Figure 10.2). It's an immense, hellish dump site, where twenty-five thousand people live and sustain themselves scavenging discards they can sell. Somehow the people of this region of the world have allowed this festering landfill to become part of their gray market. Would it not be better to layer an actual thriving economy over this mess?

---

[33] http://www.atl.com/community/sustainability/.

FIGURE 10.2. "Smokey Mountain" in Manila is famous for its constant smoldering, vibrant economy, and landslide-related deaths.

According to a recent news report,[34] there is a black market for cardboard in New York City, where it was reported that three thousand pounds of cardboard can go for as much as $150. That's five cents per pound, or five times what the University of Montana gets for its cardboard from Republic. It's unclear what the going rate for garbage is in Manila, but apparently some of what comes out of the trucks is deemed marketable by some of the scavengers.

If you live in a city, you've probably seen trucks driving around sporting 1-800-GOT-JUNK? labels. While I have not subscribed to this service myself, I think it's safe to assume that their financial model resembles that of the bottom right corner of the triangle in Figure 2.3, where the recycler makes money on both ends of the transaction. In the case of GOT JUNK? the company provides a service of helping an individual regain garage space, basement space, or attic space. Presumably, GOT JUNK? also has a network of other companies that are able to find antique shops, secondhand stores, repair shops, or recycling centers that, in turn, make cash from trash.

---

[34] http://www.havocscope.com/cardboard-theft-in-new-york-city/.

One of the more interesting ways that the entertainment industry has found to make money from waste is by interviewing families of people who have become hoarders. I believe I saw my first episode of *Hoarders* in 2011 or 2012. At first, I became uneasy as some of the piles of papers accumulating in the homes of some of the people featured on the show resembled a bit of what my garage was becoming. My sense of dignity returned when I saw the depths to which some of the people featured on the show had sunken. There were people who had food piling up in their kitchens; others kept mountains of rusty automobile carcasses with no productive fate in sight. My little jars of foil wrappers in the garage awaiting their fate suddenly seemed much less quirky.

Another company that seems to be doing quite will is Rubicon. In fact, Rubicon's founder, Nate Morris, has recently been featured in various popular magazines. By building a thriving company from some humble beginnings (little more than a truck and an idea), he's earned an international reputation in sustainable waste management. He's also on the short list to receive the Ernst & Young Entrepreneur of the Year Award.

Online Resources

All the companies discussed thus far in the chapter do have websites. Some of these companies will deal directly with individuals. Others deal with other corporations or municipalities. But still others are large but less obvious and accessible. For example, one need only spend a few minutes on the Textile Fiberspace website to realize that there is, in fact, a market for everything. Upon pursuing the site, I was even able to find an entry for single shoes! There are others, like the Plastics Recycling Marketplace (http://plasticsrecyclingmarketplace.com) that display the vast array of materials for which there are aftermarket markets. This leaves a lot of room for a lot of middlemen.

In my navigating the recycling streams of Montana, I've met and interacted with some wonderful folks. One of the recycling coordinators in Helena has provided a few additional links for those of you who would like to dive a little deeper down the proverbial rabbit hole. For example, the City of Billings, not the first city to come to mind when one thinks of sustainability, does have a private curbside business called Earth First Aid (http://www.earthfirstaid.com). Helena, the state capital, also has a private service, Helena Recycling, Inc. (http://www.helenarecycling.com).

There are also websites that serve as clearinghouses for recycling networks, such as http://tools.recyclingpartnership.org/. As we've been discussing, monetization of scrap is a challenge, and there are other resources, such as the Institute of Scrap Recycling Industries, which publishes guidelines and specifications to provide consistency and standard language. A specifications document is available for download at the Institute's website, www.isri.org. Other great online resources include recycle.net (http://recycle.net/), Resource Recycling (http://www.resource-recycling.com/), and Container Recycling Institute (http://www.container-recycling.org/). The latter also has a links page with details on buying and selling, as well as a list of material-specific trade associations. Global Recycling Network (http://www.grn.com/exchange/), Scrap Monster (http://www.scrapmonster.com), Recycle Match (http://www.recyclematch.com/marketplace), and Plastics Markets at (http://www.plasticsmarkets.org) also contain info on pricing other specific materials.

Donating Materials Locally

In Missoula, there are several options for making the best use of unwanted goods. For clothes, small appliances, toys, and various other retail items, there's Goodwill. There is also a fantastic array of pawn shops and a funky little store called Circle Square that prides itself on being the spot "where dust goes to die." Circle Square is downtown on Higgins Avenue, one of the oldest streets in Missoula. It also happens to be where seasonal parades such as St. Patrick's Day, Day of the Dead, and the homecoming parades typically launch. Circle Square is truly unique, so if you're looking for some way to revive your own downtown, start your own Circle Square and have a blast getting to know your community members. I've bought and sold several things here rather than sending them to Mount Methane. I've also bought and sold things at the Sports Exchange. Another unique and quirky little shop, Sports Exchange is located on the south side of the river just off of Higgins, in the part of town called the Hip Strip. It's just next to a shoe repair shop, and its hours are always listed with an "ish" disclaimer, reflecting the owner's laid-back lifestyle. Sure, these places aren't making a capitalistic killing, but they are contributing to a thriving little ecosystem that bucks the big box stores, a.k.a. Anywhere America, that seems to dominate our landscapes and decimate retail in small cities and towns. Do a little searching in your town for such places and start your own network. Find an empty niche in the zero-waste world? Fill it!

Local Recycling Companies

Although it is not an official recycling center, Albertson's grocery stores in Missoula do have plastic bag return bins just outside the front door. This is where I stuff the bags shown in Figure 4.3 once they are full of other plastic bags and bits of thin film plastic. The plastics that come through this little receptacle are stashed along with other thin film packaging that the store receives from their suppliers on top of their cardboard baler. Once a sufficient number of plastic bags of plastic accumulate, the staff at Albertson's makes a plastic bale and places it out with the cardboard bales to go back to corporate. In fact, I was allowed to take one of these bales and densify it into pellets that then go back into manufacturing streams or waste-to-energy streams.

Republic Services, the corporate, for-profit garbage hauler that serves Missoula and owns the landfill, also operates a recycling center on Broadway west of town. One major advantage that this corporation has over other smaller recycling firms is that it has access to the company's global network. Thus, even if the Missoula facility is not as profitable as those of other municipalities, the monopoly is still maintained. Two other ways that Republic has maintained a viable economic model for so long is that (1) the company charges extra for curbside recycling pickup, and (2) the drop-off station does not compensate its patrons for some of their materials and very small amounts for others, such as aluminum cans. So the burden of sorting falls on the curbside customer, and the burden of transportation falls on the drop-off customer.

Another good local resource for the refurbishing of appliances is Appliance Warehouse. Here, you can pick up a used clothes washer or dryer for as little as fifty dollars, drop off an old fridge, or simply stand in awe of the leftovers of civilization. I've used Appliance Warehouse frequently and have always had positive interactions with the employees.

If you live in Missoula and haven't been to The Axmen, you don't know what you're missing. If you don't live in Missoula but find yourself visiting, stop by! Walking into Axmen's Broadway store is a lot like walking into a museum. You'll find on display a vast array of old hand tools, outboard motors, and memorabilia from yesteryear at which to gawk. The Axmen also has an impressive and growing materials recovery unit. The store will pay for a variety of metals, pricing them based on current commodity values.

If you follow the beer news at all, you may have learned that Montana just surpassed Vermont for number of breweries per capita. Among them is Bayern Brewery, known for its fine array of German-style beers, as well as its bottle-washing facility. Bayern not only accepts its own bottles but will also provide a discount on its products when you return the type of bottles the brewery use—brown, unembossed, nonscrew top—in one of their twenty-four bottle brown, waxed boxes, which have been designed to be reusable as well as weather-resistant.

Goodwill receives a tremendous volume of used goods, in addition to all the clothing that it's best known for (Figure 10.3), some Goodwill stores do in fact package and commodify the various fabrics that are not in sellable condition. Another incentive for dropping off unwanted clothing at Goodwill is the receipt you will receive upon your donation for a tax deduction.

FIGURE 10.3. Photo of clothing bin from a donation center such as Goodwill.

Another icon unique to Missoula is a very special place called Freecycles. This campus not far from the Clark Fork River at the bend in First Street has helped countless children and other folks from all walks of life get their wheels under them. In fact, Freecycles may be considered a perfect model for a zero-waste campus. All bicycles that come in from donations are fixed up and given away or "sold" for a donation; stripped down for parts (wheels, forks, bearings, and so on); or, in some cases, reconfigured as bike racks or other human-powered gizmos.

Garden City Recycling and I.E. Recycling are a couple of other very small local recyclers who do curbside pickup and who are working on building collection and sorting stations for several clients in town. Given the small sizes of these operations and the fact that each has only a handful of employees, consistency of service and the total volume of materials they can handle can be an issue. But both of these companies are doing their part, however small, to move Missoula toward its landfill-free commitment.

Few recycling issues are discussed more in Missoula than what to do with all the glass. On and off, the local Target store had a large glass-recycling container that was free to the public and perhaps even served as an incentive for the recycling conscious to shop at Target. However, as of this writing, the largest and most prominent glass drop-off station is no more. Target managers said that there were too many impurities in the glass. Bottles were being placed in the container with metal caps and perhaps too much organic matter, such as lemon wedges and food residue, to be resalable on the larger markets. Management admitted in a newspaper story that, when contamination was too serious for the load to be recycled, the entire container was hauled to the landfill for road building. Regardless, with the logistics and mobile apps we currently have at our fingertips, there's really no defensible reason glass bottles cannot be sent back to their places of origin for washing and reuse. If your community has wineries or breweries, check to see if they accept bottles for reuse and then patronize those that do.

Using a model similar to that of Republic and Axmen, Pacific Steel will also accept a wide variety of metals and compensate the consumer at competitive rates. My favorite Pacific Steel story was the one where a couple of guys drove a truck onto the scales, asking that the staff quickly weigh it, crush it, and fork over the cash. When the two men failed to produce the title to the vehicle upon request, however, the authorities were notified, and the two men were prosecuted for theft.

One of the craftiest shops in town is Upcycled. This tiny shop sells crafts and jewelry made from small artifacts and bits of material that would otherwise be on their way to the landfill or recycling centers.

I have yet to research what fraction of Goodwill's artifacts and materials end up in the landfill versus what ends up back in the technosphere. If there is an industrious individual at Goodwill, I encourage him or her to begin this research and take advantage of these extensive markets.

Exercises

1. Do a little searching online or in the yellow pages for recycling centers near you. Consider volunteering or working for one.
2. Put aside some time to fix one of your favorite artifacts.
3. Build something out of waste and use it.

11

Further Steps

Well, here we are. Unlike the perpetual state of matter and energy, this little primer has an end. The atoms that comprise its structure and the energy embodied in the electrons and photons that are enabling you to process the information contained herein will continue to dance beyond all our lifetimes, but the information stream of this work is finite and nearing its conclusion.

So besides adopting the YIMBY practices spelled out at the beginning of chapter 1, what else can you do? One thing you might first do is look to your local government. Write to your mayor. Or better yet, meet with him or her to explore strategies to go landfill-free in your community.

Get to know your neighbors better and discuss joining forces and forming alliances. You'll be amazed by some of the weird stuff they're holding onto or how they were just wishing to meet someone like you with a compost pile to share. You can also share drop-off duties with your zee-dub teammates and use the proceeds for a block party.

Start your own business. You don't have to own a truck and ten acres to make a difference in sustainability. You can grab a domain name or simply hop onto an existing public site and start becoming an online recycling coordinator.

Go grab other books to learn how existing industries have sparked entire new industries. One of my favorite examples of this is Simon Garfield's *Mauve: How One Man Invented a Color That Changed the World*, which describes one scientist's successful use of waste effluent from the coal and oil industry to launch a revolution in women's clothing design[49]. Other resources include Connett's *Zero Waste Solution*[23], Beavan's *No Impact Man*[8], McDonough and Braungart's *Cradle to Cradle*[85], and Carns's *Off On Our Own*[17]. I also recommend picking up an entertaining and passionate book by my friend and colleague Craig Thomas, *Regurgitations of a Montana Forester*[131]. It was during the time that Craig was recovering from a broken hip that he invented a novel carbon capture system that we are prototyping and attempting to bring to market now.

Get creative! What can we do to maximize the utility of your own post-consumer waste? My advice here is to always aim for the *build* solution first. If the article in question is made of paper or some other natural fiber, bury it. As a last resort, burn, but only in an environmentally friendly manner and only for the purpose of making heat or ambiance.

You might also want to head to your favorite brewery to see whether or not my colleagues at COBrew have deployed their carbon capture technology yet. It's essentially a technology for keeping carbon dioxide that otherwise would leak into the atmosphere on-site for the carbonation of beer.

Another company at the leading edge of eliminating the idea of waste is PCS Biofuels out of Vancouver, British Columbia, in Canada. This team of scientists has developed a way to pull carbon and other raw materials out of conventional waste streams and put them back into industry as commodities. If you're looking for another scientific challenge on how to wrap your head around the big picture of waste, check out the Chemical-Looping Combustion Laboratory at Chalmers University of Technology in Gothenberg, Sweden. This team of researchers is looking at ways to take zero waste to the molecular level by repetitive cycling of gaseous waste products.

You should also check out the *Story of Stuff*. Having had the opportunity to meet Stiv Wilson firsthand after hearing his talk in Missoula, I know we're going to witness more great things out of this leader in the fight against plastic pollution in our waterways.

I also encourage you to think about ways to clean up your act at home. It is my vision that, before long, we are going to be turning our chimneys upside down and pumping the particulates and greenhouse gasses through biomass filters. We'll run these pumps with thermal gradients created by tubes that are heated by the sun and cooled by the Earth. If the predictions of climate change are real, we're going to need to get real ourselves and turn our homes into carbon sinks rather than carbon sources.

Let's also continue to explore the biological realm and let the microorganisms do their thing. There are more single-celled critters doing more metabolic magic at the microscale than we may ever know or understand. So let's be mindful of what the small-scale natural world is already doing to clean up our messes and amplify its efforts.

On the policy side, it's time to turn the works of thinkers like Beinhocker and Nash and doers like Leonard and Conrad and Carns into a global trend[9,17,77,91]. It's time to develop the social technologies necessary to reinternalize the streams of matter that are emitted from our homes, offices, factories, and vehicles. Before long, we'll have homes and cities that actually make the world cleaner rather than dirtier.

Exercises

1. Write down a list of resolutions you will follow based on the Quick-Start, 12-Step Guide. Include the trouble spots, listing things that will be the most challenging to recycle, and research local industries that can accept these items.
2. Go outside and do some sweeping, trash pickup, or other yard work. Force yourself to triage the things you touch into either technosphere or biosphere, with the goal of expanding the biosphere.

Appendix 1

Cost per Pound of a Few Common Materials

Table 12.1. Commodity values of common post-consumer waste. It's likely that you throw "away" about fifty pounds of this stuff per week. At an average value of three cents a pound, that's about a buck fifty a week or seventy-five dollars a year that heads to the landfill. This is at least five million dollars per year that the Last Best Place currently trashes on an annual basis. It is somewhat ironic that this is about what Republic collects in curbside fees.

Material	Value ($/lb)
paper	$0.02
HDPE	$0.04
PETE	$0.03
wood	$0.05
glass	$0.01
aluminum cans	$0.40
steel	$0.03
copper	$1.50

Appendix 2

A Little Global Warming Mathematics

As we just saw in table 12.1, Missoula pays about $5 million per year to throw "away" about $5 million worth of stuff. Are we really long enough on space and short enough on creativity in the Last Best Place to keep this up? It turns out, according to the math, that some Missoulians are actually paying about a dime per pound to have their waste driven around town for an hour or so in a fifty-ton truck that's getting a few miles per gallon while spewing carbon dioxide into the atmosphere at a rate of three to five pounds per mile, only to have that waste end up in a big heap with everyone else's stuff, where it will decay into toxic gas and toxic sludge for time immemorial.

As a very simple first-order approximation, we can in fact calculate the number of degrees that our combustion-based technologies warm the Earth with a single engineering equation and a few physical constants. The specific heat equation ($\Delta T = \Delta Q / m c_{\mathrm{p}}$) tells us that the change in temperature of a massive body, such as the atmosphere, equals the change in heat divided by the body's mass and its inherent ability to store thermal energy.[36] In this equation, ΔQ ("delta Q," or "Dee-Q") is the heating load placed on the atmosphere by humanity's technology, m is mass of the atmosphere, and c_{p} is the specific heat capacity of a substance (in this case air). Since these three numbers are well known, we can find ΔT, the annual change in temperature of the heat sink (in this case the atmosphere). With ΔQ = 500 EJ, m = 5 Zg, and c_{p} = 1 J g^{-1} K^{-1}, we arrive at

$$\Delta T = 500 \cdot 10^{18} \, \mathrm{J} \, / \, (5 \cdot 10^{21} \, \mathrm{g} \cdot 1 \, \mathrm{J} \, \mathrm{g}^{-1} \, \mathrm{K}^{-1}) = 0.1 \, \mathrm{K},$$

or one-tenth of one degree of heating of the atmosphere per year. There are, of course, other factors such as the greenhouse gas effect that accelerate this and Earth's natural radiation, which decelerates it. Readers wishing to gain an entry-level understanding of the ever-expanding world of science should read Dawkins and Wells[28,29,148].

We will never live in a world without fire. It has been and will continue to be a part of our daily lives for as long as we walk the Earth. In fact, as I'm writing this, I am putting in a proposal to build a pyrolysis machine designed to slowly and efficiently convert carbon-based waste into heat, water, and carbon dioxide. I am simultaneously submitting a proposal to further develop a biologically active filter to metabolize carbon dioxide emissions from a gaseous state into a gelatinous, living form, thus allowing combustion to continue without the side effects of unwanted emissions.

Appendix 3

Technosphere vs. Biosphere

What follows is an extension of a paper I recently published on the relationship among entropy, information, and money required to track the flow of atoms and materials in both the technosphere and the biosphere[71,72].

"Everybody wins as long as somebody loses." This occurred to me when I was feeling cynical about recycling and waste management. The concept was further brought home to me recently when I was watching one of Neil deGrasse Tyson's *Cosmos* episodes. In this particular episode, "Clean Room," Neil discussed the pioneering work of Claire Patterson on lead poisoning. The series began with his having apparent hallucinations where everything around him, including people, were getting little blotches of discoloration. As it turned out his hallucinations were real, but invisible to the naked eye.

Patterson was the first scientist to accurately predict the age of the Earth by measuring lead content in meteorites. Through his work, he also measured both the natural and anthropogenic levels of lead in the technosphere, biosphere, and terrasphere (regions of the Earth untouched by technology or biology, or the region labeled as N in Figure 1.8). After publication of his work, which revealed substantially greater levels of lead in the technosphere and the immediate biosphere than would be present if it were not for leaded gasoline, leaded paint, lead plumbing, and the like, he was approached by representatives from the petroleum industry, which was funding his research. After refusing to discontinue his lead research, Patterson sought support from federal agencies and eventually gained the ear of Congress. Ultimately, lead was deemed a contaminant, and we now use lead-free gasoline, paint, and so on. Regrettably, we are still dealing with the invisible blotches of lead as evidenced recently in Flint, Michigan.

The paradox of the win/loss paradigm should now be apparent in that everybody winning represents the reduction in the amount of lead in our immediate technosphere, thus avoiding the apparent fate of the Romans, whereas the loser is the petroleum industry. Its capitalists must now spend more on R&D and foot the bill for reengineering the manner in which combustion engines burn hydrocarbons. We are now facing a similar situation with a different molecule—$O=C=O$. Carbon dioxide is the most abundant final byproduct of every fossil fuel chemical combustion reaction. How we reengineer our transportation and energy sectors to keep carbon dioxide and other greenhouse gasses out of the atmosphere will determine whether or not we need to reengineer our coastal cities to deal with rising sea levels.

Here are a few grand challenges I would like to pose to the next generation of engineers and technologists:

1. Build a bioreactor to gasify biomaterials and biowaste. One challenge that I've found to remaining landfill-free is how to deal with food, plant, and animal waste that may contain pathogens such as bacteria or viruses. The idea here would be to heat the waste material, either with sunlight or with anaerobic waste heat or a combination of both, to turn the waste into gasses that can then be burned for energy, bottled for commercial sale, or released into a greenhouse.

2. Do a chemical analysis on the effluent from a wastewater treatment plant or flue gas stack in your community. What is actually going into the water we drink and the air we breathe? Become a citizen scientist!

3. Build a waste stream separator for household vacuum bags. The idea here is that the contents of a bag would be emptied into a chamber that is likely full of water and a series of filters that reclaim materials by size, density, and ultimately material type. Valuable artifacts such as earrings, coins, Legos, and the like, are recovered; synthetic materials such as carpet fragments, bits of plastic, and so on, are triaged for recycling; and biomaterials are triaged for composting or for a bioreactor.

References

[1]   American Society for Testing and Materials. 1994. *ASTM Standards and Other Specifications and Test Methods on the Quality Assurance of Landfill Liner Systems*. Philadelphia, PA.

[2]   Amundson, R., A. A. Berhe, J. W. Hopmans, C. Olson, A. E. Sztein, and D. L. Sparks. 2015. "Soil Science. Soil and Human Security in the 21st Century." *Science* 348 (6235): 1261071.

[3]   Anonymous. 1910. "A Hand-Axe Found 'in situ' in Natal." *Anthropologie* 21 (4): 541–42.

[4]   Bailey, G. 1995. "The Balkans in Prehistory: The Paleolithic Archaeology of Greece and Adjacent Areas." *Antiquity* 69 (262): 19–24.

[5]   Bailey, R. 2015. *The End of Doom: Environmental Renewal in the Twenty-first Century*. New York: St. Martin's Press.

[6]   Baum, B., C. H. Parker, A. J. Warner, Debell and Richardson Inc., and Manufacturing Chemists' Association (US). 1972. *Plastics Waste Disposal Practices in Landfill, Incineration, Pyrolysis, and Recycle*. Washington, Manufacturing Chemists Association.

[7]   Baxter, S. 2005. "A Human Galaxy: A Prehistory of the Future." *Jbis-Journal of the British Interplanetary Society* 58 (3–4): 138–42.

[8]   Beavan, C. 2009. *No Impact Man: The Adventures of a Guilty Liberal Who Attempts to Save the Planet, and the Discoveries He Makes about Himself and Our Way of Life in the Process*. New York: Macmillan.

[9]   Beinhocker, E. D. 2006. *The Origin of Wealth: Evolution, Complexity, and the Radical Remaking of Economics*. Boston, MA. Harvard Business School Press.

[10]   Bendall, J. G. 2007. "Food Contamination with Styrene Dibromide via Packaging Migration of Leachate from Polystyrene Cold-Storage Insulation." *Journal of Food Protection* 70 (4): 1,037–40.

[11]   Boyle, G. 2004. *Renewable Energy Power for a Sustainable Future.* Oxford University Press.

[12]   Brown, D. and E. Herrmann. 2013. *The Boys in the Boat: Nine Americans and their Epic Quest for Gold at the 1936 Berlin Olympics.* New York: Penguin Audio.

[13]   Calheiros, C. S. C., A. Rangel, and P. M. L. Castro. 2014. "Constructed Wetlands for Tannery Wastewater Treatment in Portugal: Ten Years of Experience." *International Journal of Phytoremediation* 16 (9): 859–70.

[14]   California Integrated Waste Management Board and GeoSyntec Consultants. 2004. *Landfill Facility Compliance Study Phase II Report: Evaluation of Regulatory Effectiveness Based on a Review of 53 MSW Landfills.* Sacramento, CA, California Environmental Protection Agency, Integrated Waste Management Board.

[15]   Campbell, J. 1990. *Transformations of Myth through Time.* New York: Perennial Library.

[16]   Canfield, T. J., N. E. Kemble, W. G. Brumbaugh, F. J. Dwyer, C. G. Ingersoll, and J. F. Fairchild. 1994. "Use of Benthic Invertebrate Community Structure and the Sediment Quality Triad to Evaluate Metal-Contaminated Sediment in the Upper Clark-Fork River, Montana." *Environmental Toxicology and Chemistry* 13 (12): 1999–2012.

[17]   Carns, T. 2011. *Off on Our Own: Living Off-Grid in Comfortable Independence.* Pittsburgh: St. Lynns Press.

[18]   Carvalho, P. N., M. C. P. Basto, C. M. R. Almeida, and H. Brix. 2014. "A Review of Plant-Pharmaceutical Interactions: From Uptake and Effects in Crop Plants to Phytoremediation in Constructed Wetlands." *Environmental Science and Pollution Research* 21 (20): 11,729–763.

[19]   Cavanagh, T. E., and Illinois Environmental Protection Agency. 1973. *Sanitary Landfill Management.* Springfield, Illinois, Environmental Protection Agency.

[20]   Chaisson, E. 2001. *Cosmic Evolution: The Rise of Complexity in Nature.* Cambridge, MA. Harvard University Press.

[21]   Christian, D. 2008. *This Fleeting World: A Short History of Humanity.* Great Barrington, MA. Berkshire Pub.

[22]   Christian, D. 2011. "David Christian: The History of Our World in 18 Minutes," TED Talks. https://www.ted.com/talks/ david_christian_big_history

[23]   Connett, P. H. 2013. *The Zero Waste Solution: Untrashing the Planet One Community at a Time.* White River Junction, Vermont: Chelsea Green Publishing.

[24]   Copyright Collection (Library of Congress). 2007. *The World without Us: A Documentary.*

[25]   Cornwall, P. B. 1946. "A Lower Paleolithic Hand-Axe from Central Arabia." *Man* 46 (6): 144.

[26]   Dadrasnia, A., I. Salmah, C. U. Emenike, and N. Shahsavari. 2015. "Remediation of Oil Contaminated Media Using Organic Material Supplementation." *Petroleum Science and Technology* 33 (9): 1030-37.

[27]   Davis, T., and S. Light. 2014. "Duke Energy Apologizes for Dan River Ash Spill." Star Tribune.

[28]   *Dawkins, R. 1976. The Selfish Gene.* New York: Oxford University Press.

[29]   Dawkins, R. 2004. *The Ancestor's Tale: A Pilgrimage to the Dawn of Evolution.* Boston: Houghton Mifflin.

[30]   Delbrück, M. 1985. *Mind from Matter?* Blackwell Pub.

[31]   Despriee, J., P. Voinchet, R. Gageonnet, J. Depont, J. J. Bahain, C. Falgueres, H. Tissoux, J. M. Dolo, and G. Courcimault. 2009. "The Earliest Human Populating during the Lower and Middle Pleistocene in the Middle Basin of the Loire River, Centre Region, France. First Results of the Studies of the Fluvial Formations." *Anthropologie* 113 (1): 125–67.

[32]   Diamond, J. M. 1997. *Guns, Germs, and Steel: The Fates of Human Societies.* New York: W.W. Norton & Co.

[33]   Diamond, J. M. 2005. *Collapse: How Societies Choose to Fail or Succeed.* New York: Viking.

[34]   Dusterhoff, H. L., P. M. Norbeck, and K. Miller. 1998. "Evaluation of Non-Point Source Pollution and Land Uses in the Red River

Watershed in Glacier and Toole Counties, Montana." *Abstracts of Papers of the American Chemical Society* 215: U235–U235.

[35]   Enders, K., R. Lenz, C. A. Stedmon, and T. G. Nielsen. 2015. "Abundance, Size and Polymer Composition of Marine Microplastics >= 10 mm in the Atlantic Ocean and their Modelled Vertical Distribution." *Marine Pollution Bulletin* 100 (1): 70–81.

[36]   Engineering Toolbox. 2015. Specific Heat. http://www.engineeringtoolbox.com/heat-capacity-d 338.html

[37]   Environment Australia. 1999. Incineration and Dioxins: Review of Formation Processes, Consultancy Report Prepared by Environmental and Safety Services for Environment Australia.

[38]   European Environment Agency. 2009. *Diverting Waste from Landfill: effectiveness of Waste-Management Policies in the European Union.* Luxembourg: Office for Official Publications of the European Communities.

[39]   Everett, R., G. Boyle, S. Peake, and J. Ramage. 2012. *Energy Systems and Sustainability: Power for a Sustainable Future.* Oxford: Oxford University Press.

[40]   Feng, X. B. 2008. "Technological Characterization of China and Europe Lower Paleolithic Industry from 1 Ma to 400,000 Years: Similarity and Difference between the Yunxian Hominid Culture and European Acheulean." *Anthropologie* 112 (3): 423–47.

[41]   Fernando, A. L., M. P. Duarte, A. Vatsanidou, and E. Alexopoulou. 2015. "Environmental Aspects of Fiber Crops Cultivation and Use." *Industrial Crops and Products* 68: 105–115.

[42]   Fischer, D., Y. X. Li, B. Ahlemeyer, J. Krieglstein, and T. Kissel. 2003. "In Vitro Cytotoxicity Testing of Polycations: Influence of Polymer Structure on Cell Viability and Hemolysis." *Biomaterials* 24 (7): 1121–31.

[43]   Flores, H. C. 2006. *Food Not Lawns: How to Turn Your Yard into a Garden and Your Neighborhood into a Community.* White River Junction, VT: Chelsea Green Pub. Company.

[44]   Foroohar, R. 2016. "Saving Capitalism." *Time* May (23): 26–32.

[45]   Fox. 2013. "Top NASA Scientist Arrested (Again) in White House Protest." http://www.foxnews.com/science/2013/02/13/top-nasa-climate-scientist-arrested-again-in-white-house-protest.html

[46]   Francis, J. M. B. 2015. "Encyclical Letter Laudato Si' of the Holy
        Father Francis on Care for Our Common Home." The Vatican.

[47]   Friedman, T. L. 2008. *Hot, Flat, and Crowded: Why We Need a Green
        Revolution – And How It Can Renew America*. New York: Farrar,
        Straus and Giroux.

[48]   Gall, J. E., R. S. Boyd, and N. Rajakaruna. 2015. "Transfer of Heavy
        Metals through Terrestrial Food Webs: A review." *Environmental
        Monitoring and Assessment* 187 (4).

[49]   Garfield, S. 2001. *Mauve*. W.W. Norton & Co.

[50]   Garcia-Rodriguez, A., V. Matamoros, C. Fontas, and V. Salvado.
        2014. "The Ability of Biologically Based Wastewater Treatment
        Systems to Remove Emerging Organic Contaminants-A Review."
        Environmental Science and Pollution Research 21 (20): 11708–728.

[51]   Genet, R. 1997. *The Chimpanzees Who Would Be Ants: The
        Evolutionary Epic of Humanity*. Commack, NY: Nova Science
        Publications.

[52]   Glass, P., and F. F. Coppola. 1982. *Koyaanisqatsi: Life Out of Balance*.
        https://www.youtube.com/watch?v=PirH8PADDgQ

[53]   Goldwasser, S., M. Sudan, and V. Vaikuntanathan. 2005.
        "Distributed Computing with Imperfect Randomness." *Distributed
        Computing, Proceedings*. P. Fraigniaud. Berlin, Springer-Verlag
        Berlin. 3724: 288–302.

[54]   Gomez-Sagasti, M. T., and D. Marino. 2015. "PGPRs and
        Nitrogen-Fixing Legumes: A Perfect Team for Efficient Cd
        Phytoremediation?" *Frontiers in Plant Science* 6.

[55]   Gregory, M. E., and S. James. 2009. *Toilets of the World*. London,
        New York: Merrell.

[56]   Gupta, D. K., S. Chatterjee, S. Datta, V. Veer, and C. Walther.
        2014. Role of Phosphate Fertilizers in Heavy Metal Uptake and
        Detoxification of Toxic Metals." *Chemosphere* 108: 134–44.

[57]   Gurrieri, J. T. 1998. "Distribution of Metals in Water and Sediment
        and Effects on Aquatic Biota in the upper Stillwater River Basin,
        Montana." *Journal of Geochemical Exploration* 64 (1–3): 83–100.

[58]   Harari, Y. N. 2015. *Sapiens: A Brief History of Humankind*. New
        York: HarperCollins Publishers.

[59]   He, F., J. Gao, E. Pierce, P. J. Strong, H. L. Wang, and L. Y. Liang. 2015. "In Situ Remediation Technologies for Mercury-Contaminated Soil." *Environmental Science and Pollution Research* 22 (11): 8124–147.

[60]   Iqbal, M., A. Ahmad, M. K. A. Ansari, M. I. Qureshi, I. M. Aref, P. R. Khan, S. S. Hegazy, H. El-Atta, A. Husen, and K. R. Hakeem. 2015. "Improving the Phytoextraction Capacity of Plants to Scavenge Metal (Loid)-Contaminated Sites." *Environmental Reviews* 23 (1): 44–65.

[61]   Josselyn, D. W. 1967. "Does America Have a Hand Axe?" *Anthropological Journal of Canada* 5 (1): 27–29.

[62]   Kang, S., S. W. Running, J. S. Kimball, D. B. Fagre, A. Michaelis, D. L. Peterson, J. E. Halofsky, and S. Hong. 2014. "Effects of Spatial and Temporal Climatic Variability on Terrestrial Carbon and Water Fluxes in the Pacific Northwest, USA." *Environmental Modelling & Software* 51: 228–39.

[63]   Kolbert, E. 2006. *Field Notes from a Catastrophe: Man, Nature, and Climate Change.* New York, Bloomsbury Pub. Holtzbrinck Publishers.

[64]   Koptsik, G. N. 2014. "Problems and Prospects Concerning the Phytoremediation of Heavy Metal Polluted Soils: A Review." *Eurasian Soil Science* 47 (9): 923–39.

[65]   Krakauer, J. 2014. *Missoula: Rape and the Justice System in a College Town.*

[66]   Lalman. 1978. "Hand-Axe: New Discovery in Ghaggar-Nalagarh Complex." *Current Science* 47 (17): 629–30.

[67]   Layton, B. E. 2008. "A Comparison of Energy Densities of Prevalent Energy Sources in Units of Joules per Cubic Meter." *International Journal of Green Energy* 5: 438–55.

[68]   Layton, B. E. 2011. "The Role of Mechanoevolution in Predicting the Future of Micro- and Nanoscale Technologies." *Systems Engineering for Microscale and Nanoscale Technologies.* M. A. G. Darrin and J. Barth. Boca Raton, FL: CRC Press.

[69]   Layton, B. E. 2011. "The Application of Game Theory to Thermoeconomics." Proceedings of the ASME 2011 International

Mechanical Engineering Congress and Exhibition, Denver, Colorado.

[70] Layton, B. E. 2012. "Mechanoevolution: An Examination of the Coevolution of Humans and Technology". Inaugural Meeting of the International Big History Association, Grand Rapids, MI, USA.

[71] Layton, B. E. 2014. *"Anthropogenic Entropy Acceleration and Its Relationship to Shannon Information in the Context of Socioeconomics."* Energy and Sustainability. Putrajaya, Malaysia: WIT Press.

[72] Layton, B. E. S.L Noell & G.A. Oram JR. 2016. "Entropy Acceleration, Shannon Information and Socioeconomics: Quantitative Examples" International Journal of Design & Nature and Ecodynamics 11 (1) 48-63.

[73] Le Quere, C., M. Raupach, J. Canadell, G. Marland, L. Bopp, P. Ciais, T. Conway, S. Doney, R. Feely, P. Foster, P. Friedlingstein, K. Gurney, R. Houghton, J. House, C. Huntingford, P. Levy, M. Lomas, J. Majkut, N. Metzl, J. Ometto, G. Peters, I. Prentice, J. Randerson, S. Running, J. Sarmiento, U. Schuster, S. Sitch, T. Takahashi, N. Viovy, G. van der Werf, and F. Woodward. 2009. "Trends in the Sources and Sinks of Carbon Dioxide." *Nature Geoscience*: 831–36.

[74] Leakey, L. S. B. 1973. "Was Homo-Erectus Responsible for Hand-Axe Culture?" *Journal of Human Evolution* 2 (6): 493–98.

[75] Leeper, A. 2004. *Landfill*. Chicago, IL: Heinemann Library.

[76] Lehmann, E. C. 2007. *Landfill Research Focus*. New York: Nova Science Publishers.

[77] Leonard, A., and A. Conrad. 2010. *The Story of Stuff: How Our Obsession with Stuff Is Trashing the Planet, Our Communities, and Our Health—and a Vision for Change*. New York: Free Press.

[78] Lovins, A. B. 2011. *Reinventing Fire: Bold Business Solutions for the New Energy Era*. White River Junction, VT. Chelsea Green Pub.

[79] Lusher, A. L., V. Tirelli, I. O'Connor, and R. Officer. 2015. "Microplastics in Arctic Polar Waters: The First Reported Values of Particles in Surface and Sub-Surface Samples." *Scientific Reports* 5.

[80] Mahmoudi, M., A. Simchi, H. Vali, M. Imani, M. A. Shokrgozar, K. Azadmanesh, and F. Azari. 2009. "Cytotoxicity and Cell Cycle Effects of Bare and Poly (vinyl alcohol)-Coated Iron Oxide

Nanoparticles in Mouse Fibroblasts." *Advanced Engineering Materials* 11 (12): B243–B250.

[81] Mannchen, J. 2001. "The German Tool Museum of Remscheid: Treasures of the Technical History of Civilization – from Hand-Axe to CNC Tool." *Stahl Und Eisen* 121 (6): 119–20.

[82] Manning, R. 2004. *Against the Grain*. North Point Press.

[83] Mavropoulos, A. 2013. *Waste Atlas*. https://www.witpress.com/Secure/ejournals/papers/DNE110106f.pdf

[84] McDonald, A. 2012 *Truth, Lies, and O-Rings: Inside the Space Shuttle Challenger Disaster*. University Press of Florida.

[85] McDonough, W., and M. Braungart. 2002. *Cradle to Cradle: Remaking the Way We Make Things*. New York: North Point Press.

[86] McWilliams, J. R. 1959. *Mining methods and costs at the Anaconda Company Berkeley Pit, Butte, MT*. Washington, U. S. Dept. of the Interior, Bureau of Mines.

[87] Menikpura, S. N. M., J. Sang-Arun, and M. Bengtsson. 2013. "Integrated Solid Waste Management: An Approach for Enhancing Climate Co-Benefits through Resource Recovery." *Journal of Cleaner Production* 58: 34–42.

[88] Mildenberger, G. 1958. "Hand-Axe and Bronze Sword – Prehistoric Research in Northern Europe – Bibby, G." *Historische Zeitschrift* 186 (3): 597–98.

[89] Moir, J. R. 1931. "A Hand-Axe from the Upper Chalky Boulder Clay." *Man* 31 (1): 7–9.

[90] Moir, J. R. 1932. "A Primitive Transitional Hand-Axe from beneath the Red Crag." *Man* 32 (3): 61–63.

[91] Nash, J. 1950. "The Bargaining Problem." *Econometrica* 18 (2): 155–62.

[92] New Zealand, Ministry for the Environment. 2004. *Landfill Full Cost Accounting Guide for New Zealand*. Wellington, NZ: Ministry for the Environment.

[93] Newman, W. A., and W. E. Holton. 2006. *Boston's Back Bay: The Story of America's Greatest Nineteenth-Century Landfill Project*. Boston: Northeastern University Press.

[94] Nimick, D. A., and J. N. Moore. 1991. "Prediction of Water-Soluble Metal Concentrations in Fluvially Deposited Tailings Sediments,

Upper Clark Fork Valley, Montana, USA." *Applied Geochemistry* 6 (6): 635–46.

[95] Nuffer, J. R., T. M. Harper, and California Integrated Waste Management Board. 1992. *Reaching the Limit: An Interim Report on Landfill Capacity in California: A Compilation of County Local Task Force Findings as of January 1, 1990.* Sacramento (8800 Cal Center Drive, Sacramento 95826): California Integrated Waste Management Board.

[96] Oliveira, V., N. C. M. Gomes, A. Almeida, A. M. S. Silva, H. Silva, and A. Cunha. 2015. "Microbe-Assisted Phytoremediation of Hydrocarbons in Estuarine Environments." *Microbial Ecology* 69 (1): 1–12.

[97] Ontario Ministry of Environment and Energy. 1993. *Guidance Manual for Landfill Sites Receiving Municipal Waste.* Ontario: Ministry of Environment and Energy.

[98] Otto, B., and H. Obermaier. 1909. "An 'in situ' Discovered Hand Axe from Natal." *Anthropos* 4 (5–6): 972–75.

[99] Padmavathiamma, P. K., M. Ahmed, and H. A. Rahman. 2014. "Phytoremediation: A Sustainable Approach for Contaminant Remediation in Arid and Semi-Arid Regions –a Review." *Emirates Journal of Food and Agriculture* 26 (9): 757–72.

[100] Perry, G. H., L. Kistler, M. A. Kelaita, and A. J. Sams. 2015. "Insights into Hominin Phenotypic and Dietary Evolution from Ancient DNA Sequence Data." *Journal of Human Evolution* 79: 55–63.

[101] Petroski, H. 1992. *The Evolution of Useful Things.* New York: Knopf.

[102] Pollan, M. 2006. *The Omnivore's Dilemma: A Natural History of Four Meals.* New York: Penguin Press.

[103] Poulton, B. C., D. P. Monda, D. F. Woodward, M. L. Wildhaber, and W. G. Brumbaugh. 1995. "Relations between Benthic Community Structure and Metals Concentrations in Aquatic Macroinvertebrates – Clark-Fork Montana." *Journal of Freshwater Ecology* 10 (3): 277–93.

[104] Prigogine, I. 1990. "The Behavior of Matter under Nonequilibrium Conditions: Fundamental Aspects and Applications." Department of Energy Progress Report.

[105] R.W. Beck and Associates and R. Moeller. 1995. Madison County landfill, Madison County, Indiana: March, 1995. Columbus, Neb., Beck and Associates.

[106] Rajaram, V., F. Z. Siddiqui, and M. Emran Khan. 2012. *From Landfill Gas to Energy: Technologies and Challenges.* Leiden, The Netherlands; New York: CRC/Balkema.

[107] Richter, J. 2013. "The Homo Heidelbergensis and Conscious Geometrical Design? Analysis of the Production Process of a Hand Axe from Bad Salzuflen (East Westphalia-Lippe)." *Archaologisches Korrespondenzblatt* 43 (1): 1–17.

[108] Robinson, B. H., C. W. N. Anderson, and N. M. Dickinson. 2015. "Phytoextraction: Where's the action?" *Journal of Geochemical Exploration* 151: 34–40.

[109] Rothrock, J. A., P. K. Barten, and G. L. Ingman. 1998. "Land Use and Aquatic Biointegrity in the Blackfoot River Watershed, Montana." *Journal of the American Water Resources Association* 34 (3): 565–81.

[110] Roy, M., A. K. Giri, S. Dutta, and P. Mukherjee. 2015. "Integrated Phytobial Remediation for Sustainable Management of Arsenic in Soil and Water." *Environment International* 75: 180–98.

[111] Running, S. W. 2006. "Is Global Warming Causing More, Larger Wildfires?" *Science* 313 (5,789): 927–28.

[112] Sachs, J. 2012. *The Price of Civilization: Reawakening American Virtue and Prosperity.* New York: Random House Trade Paperbacks.

[113] Schramski, J. R., D. K. Gattie, and J. H. Brown. 2015. "Human Domination of the Biosphere: Rapid Discharge of the Earth-Space Battery Foretells the Future of Humankind." *PNAS* 112 (31): 9,511–517.

[114] Schrödinger, E. 1944, 2012. *What Is Life? The Physical Aspect of the Living Cell & Mind and Matter* Cambridge; New York: Cambridge University Press.

[115] Schumacher, M. M., and Johns Hopkins University, Applied Physics Laboratory. 1983. *Landfill Methane Recovery.* Park Ridge, NJ: Noyes Data Corp.

[116] Scott, G. R., and L. Gibert. 2009. "The oldest hand-axes in Europe." *Nature* 461 (7,260): 82–85.

[117] Seddon, D. 1966. "Function of Hand-Axe." *Man* 1 (2): 244.

[118]   Senior, E. 1995. *Microbiology of Landfill Sites*. Boca Raton: Lewis
         Publishers.

[119]   San Francisco Environment. 2015. "Mandatory Recycling and
         Composting Ordinance."

[120]   Sherman, P., and E. van Sebille. 2016. "Modeling Marine Surface
         Microplastic Transport to Assess Optimal Removal Locations."
         Environmental Research Letters 11 (1).

[121]   Smith, G. R. 2015. "Phytoremediation-By-Design: Community-
         Scale Landscape Systems Design for Healthy Communities."
         International Journal of Sustainable Development and World Ecology
         22 (5): 413–19.

[122]   Solid Waste Association of North America, Landfill Gas Division.
         1993. *A Compilation of Landfill Gas Field Practices and Procedures*.
         Silver Spring, MD: Solid Waste Association of North America.

[123]   SPREP. 2010. *A Practical Guide to Landfill Management in Pacific
         Island Countries and Territories*. Apia, Samoa: SPREP.

[124]   Stationary Office. 2006. *Reducing the Reliance on Landfill in England:
         Department for Environment, Food and Rural Affairs*. London:
         Stationery Office.

[125]   Sturm, J. 2011. *Filling the Earth with Trash*. Vero Beach, FL:
         Rourke Pub.

[126]   Suplee, M. W., V. Watson, W. K. Dodds, and C. Shirley. 2012.
         "Response of Algal Biomass to Large-Scale Nutrient Controls in the
         Clark Fork River, Montana, United States." *Journal of the American
         Water Resources Association* 48 (5): 1,008–1,021.

[127]   Tainter, J. 1990. *Collapse of Complex Societies*. Cambridge University
         Press.

[128]   Tainter, J. 2012b. Why Societies Collapse – And What It Means
         for Us

[129]   Tang, W. C., I. Hemm, and G. Eisenbrand. 2000. "Estimation of
         Human Exposure to Styrene and Ethylbenzene." *Toxicology* 144
         (1–3): 39–50.

[130]   Taylor, A. K., J. K. Stein, and Burke Museum of Natural History and
         Culture. 2011. *Is It a House? Archaeological Excavations at English
         Camp, San Juan Island, Washington*. Seattle, WA: Burke Museum;
         distributed by University of Washington Press.

[131]   Thomas, C. E. 2009. *Regurgitations of a Montana Forester.* Stevensville, MT, Stoneydale Press Pub. Co.

[132]   Thomson, V. E. 2009. *Garbage In, Garbage Out: Solving the Problems with Long-Distance Trash Transport.* Charlottesville: University of Virginia Press.

[133]   Ullah, A., S. Heng, M. F. H. Munis, S. Fahad, and X. Y. Yang. 2015. "Phytoremediation of Heavy Metals Assisted by Plant Growth Promoting (PGP) Bacteria: A Review." *Environmental and Experimental Botany* 117: 28–40.

[134]   Umeji, O. P., A. M. Ibeanu, and C. O. C. Agwu. 2012. "Holocene Human Occupation of the Eastern Nigerian Scarp Lands: An Impact Assessment Study." *Quaternary International* 262: 2–13.

[135]   United States Consumer Protection and Environmental Health Service Environmental Control Administration. 1968. *Sanitary Landfill: A Bibliography.* Washington.

[136]   Valentino, F., M. Leuenberger, C. Uglietti, and P. Staburm. 2008. "Measurements and Trend Analysis of O_2, CO_2, and D13C of CO_2 from High Altitude Research Station Junfgraujoch, Switzerland – A Comparison with the Observations from the Remote Site Puy de Dôme, France." *Science of the Total Environment*: 203–210.

[137]   Van Oosten, M. J., and A. Maggio. 2015. "Functional Biology of Halophytes in the Phytoremediation of Heavy Metal Contaminated Soils." *Environmental and Experimental Botany* 111: 135–46.

[138]   van Sebille, E., C. Wilcox, L. Lebreton, N. Maximenko, B. D. Hardesty, J. A. van Franeker, M. Eriksen, D. Siegel, F. Galgani, and K. L. Law. 2015. "A Global Inventory of Small Floating Plastic Debris." *Environmental Research Letters* 10 (12).

[139]   Vance, A. 2015. *Elon Musk: Tesla, SpaceX, and the Quest for a Fantastic Future.* New York: Ecco.

[140]   Velinni, A. A. 2007. *Landfill Research Trends.* New York: Nova Science Publishers.

[141]   Walker, M. J., M. Lopez-Martinez, J. S. Carrion-Garcia, T. Rodriguez-Estrella, M. S. N. del-Toro, J. L. Schwenninger, A. Lopez-Jimenez, J. Ortega-Rodriguez, M. Haber-Uriarte, J. L. Polo-Camacho, J. Garcia-Torres, M. Campillo-Boj, A. Aviles-Fernandez, and W. Zack. 2013. "Cueva Negra del Estrecho del Rio Quipar (Murcia, Spain):

A late Early Pleistocene Hominin Site with an 'Acheulo-Levalloiso-Mousteroid' Paleolithic assemblage." *Quaternary International* 294: 135–59.

[142]   Warner, A. J., C. H. Parker, B. Baum, Debell and Richardson Inc., and Manufacturing Chemists' Association (US). 1971. *Plastics Solid Waste Disposal by Incineration or Landfill.* Washington Manufacturing Chemists' Association.

[143]   van Haaren, R, N. Themelis, and N. Goldstein. 2008. "17th Nationwide Survey of MSW Management in the US: The State of Garbage in America," June 28, 2016 https://www.biocycle.net/images/art/1010/bc101016_s.pdf

[144]   Wikipedia "2015 Indian Heat Wave," accessed July 2, 2015, https://en.wikipedia.org/wiki/2015_Indian_heat_wave.

[145]   Weber, T. 1980. "A Hand-Axe from Magdeburg-Fermersleben." *Ausgrabungen Und Funde* 25 (4): 171–74.

[146]   Weisman, A. 2007. *The World without Us.* New York: Thomas Dunne Books / St. Martin's Press.

[147]   Weisman, A. 2008. *Gaviotas: A Village to Reinvent the World.* White River Junction, VT: Chelsea Green Pub. Co.

[148]   Wells, S., and M. Read. 2002. *The Journey of Man: A Genetic Odyssey.* Princeton, NJ: Princeton University Press.

[149]   Wernick, I. K., and J. H. Ausubel. 1995. "National Material Metrics for Industrial Ecology." *Resources Policy* 21 (3): 189–98.

[150]   Yesiller, N., J. L. Hanson, J. T. Cox, and D. E. Noce. 2014. "Determination of Specific Gravity of Municipal Solid Waste." *Waste Management* 34: 848–58.

[151]   Zhang, H. J., Y. Y. Kuo, A. C. Gerecke, and J. Wang. 2012. "Co-Release of Hexabromocyclododecane (HBCD) and Nano- and Microparticles from Thermal Cutting of Polystyrene Foams." *Environmental Science & Technology* 46 (20): 10,990–996.

Glossary

artifacts. Things built by humans from one or more materials to perform a purpose. Examples are limitless but include shovels, automobiles, eyeglasses, and coffee cups.

biosphere. All the matter that is presently alive and serves as fuel or other raw materials to support living matter. Examples include birds, compost piles, swamps with life in them, and on and on.

carbon-negative. Activities, practices, or polices that "bend down" the Keeling Curve by removing carbon compounds such as carbon dioxide and methane from the atmosphere.

chemical looping combustion. This technology is zero-waste at the molecular scale. All combustion or reaction products in a chemical looping combustion system are either consumed to produce energy, or are collected as commodities.

collapse. The point at which a system no longer functions as it originally performed. This concept can be applied to physical objects or economies or to social, legal, or business contracts.

combustion technologies. Any technology designed to burn matter for the purpose of making electricity, making heat, eliminating waste, or some combination thereof.

embodied energy. The primary energy that was used to create a pure substance, create an artifact, transport a commodity, or some combination thereof.

entropy/entropicize. The act of creating disorder. The second law of thermodynamics dictates that the order in the universe on average will diminish with time. The act of pollution accelerates the rate at which the earth becomes polluted or disordered.

EROEI. Energy returned on energy invested. For example, a process that requires more energy to produce and refine a fuel is not thermodynamically sustainable and will ultimately prove to be economically unsustainable.

fermentation. The use of microorganisms such as yeast to convert larger hydrocarbons such as glucose into fuels such as ethanol.

gasification. Heating a solid, liquid, or slurry in the absence of oxygen for the purpose of driving off gasses such as steam, carbon monoxide, methane or other fuels or commodities.

hand axes. One of the, if not the first, predominant artifacts created by humans, likely used for hunting, rudimentary agriculture, food preparation, and perhaps defense.

hydrocarbons (CxHx). Any material comprised of carbon and hydrogen. Common examples include methane, CH_4; octane, C_8H_{18}; or polyethylene, C_xH_{2x}.

incineration. Heating waste in the presence of oxygen to extract 100% of the chemical energy.

landfill-negative. Activities, practices, or policies that result in smaller landfills and ultimately the complete absence of landfills.

landfull. The author's play on words to describe the current state of our growing landfill dilemma.

material recovery facility. An alternative to a landfill, where materials are returned to the technosphere or biosphere, rather than heading to the landfill.

materials. Substances comprised of single elements such as, for example, gold or iron or substances comprised as chemical compounds for the purpose of being turned into artifacts. For example, the material steel may be turned into a nail artifact. The material plastic may be turned into artifacts such as chairs, tools, toys, and much more.

middens. Ancient landfills produced by tribal civilizations, typically containing shells, bones, and other discarded waste from meals.

net-positive. A building, piece of real estate, or other geographical location that produces more of a commodity such as food, electricity, water, or soil than it consumes.

perpetual motion. While impossible at the scale we occupy, perpetual motion is inevitable at the molecular scale. As long as temperature and pressure gradients (differences) exist in the universe, all things in the universe will continue to move.

phytoremediation. The use of plants to clean waste streams. For example, switchgrass is commonly used to clean soil and water contaminated with lead. Trees and algae "clean" the air of excess carbon dioxide.

primary energy. Energy derived directly from nature without technological intervention. Examples include fossil fuels, sunlight, and wind (including waves), as well as tidal, geothermal, and nuclear energy.

pyrolysis. heating at solid or liquid in the absence of oxygen at 200 to 300 °C (390 to 570 °F) to produce gasses such as hydrogen and methane as well as liquid tars and solid pure carbon

technosphere. Spaces built by humans to create a comfortable way of life and to support commerce. Examples include our homes, offices, and vehicles, as well as our gadgets themselves.

thermal facility. A power plant or power technology designed to either concentrate or create heat through combustion, sunlight, high-temperature geothermal sites, or nuclear fusion.

torrefaction. A "gentle" pyrolysis used to enhance fuel quality.

trash can liner. Typically a thin film plastic bag used to maintain a barrier between waste products and the waste container. In a zero-waste model, trash can liners can become obsolete or can be used in a manner in which the liners themselves enter a waste-to-energy stream.

triage/triaging. Separating a single stream of artifacts or materials into two or more streams.

YIMBY. The author's counterexample to NIMBY (not in my backyard). By accepting a "yes in my backyard" philosophy and set of practices, a zero-waste lifestyle is more comfortably achieved.

About the Author

B radley Edward Layton, PhD, PE, grew up in Seymour, Indiana. He earned a doctorate in biomedical engineering and a master's in mechanical engineering from the University of Michigan, and an SB in mechanical engineering from the Massachusetts Institute of Technology. He taught mechanical engineering courses at Drexel University in Philadelphia before joining Missoula College in Montana, where he directed the Energy Technology Program. He lives in the Rattlesnake Valley in Missoula where he serves as a licensed professional engineer, and CEO of Integration Energy LLC.

Index

Made in the USA
Middletown, DE
13 January 2019